MW01629271

What people say about this book.

Deep Excellence: Seeing and hearing a culture of deep excellence *comes at a time when the need for sustainability in organizations is greater than ever before. I was thoroughly impressed by the insights and practical advice it provides. The book delves into the various challenges that organizations face when improving culture and performance and offers concrete strategies for addressing them. I also appreciate the book's focus on the role of leadership. It shows how the systems and processes in place within an organization can either support or undermine the culture you are trying to build. By understanding the impact of these systems, leaders can make more informed decisions about how to design and implement them in a way that supports the culture they want to create.*

Overall, I would highly recommend this book to anyone looking to improve their organization's performance in a sustainable way. It offers valuable insights and practical guidance for achieving excellence. This book is a timely and valuable resource that should not be missed.

Lacey Garner, Program Manager, Central Operations IRI, United States.

'Thanks again for the opportunity to review this. Let me start with: this output is more concrete evidence that you truly are a Renaissance Man! The depth and breadth of the content is impressive. It does flow well given that almost every chapter has content that could be explored individually over a lifetime of work.

..the chapters outlining behaviors and communication (Voiceprint) resonated with me as we have been chopping wood on both of those at TIDI. A humbling reminder of asking questions out of sheer curiosity, not telling. Your overview of them was a sobering reminder for me on the tremendous discipline it takes to learn and model those behaviors. The comment you made during our time together of "what would the video look like?" has stayed with me. We now have much more insight confirming that behaviors certainly are visual and observable.'

Kevin McNamara, President and Chief Executive Officer of TIDI **Products, LLC.**

What people say about this book.

'All the organisations that I have worked with? over the last 40 years have struggled with communication, and getting a deep understanding of problems and their sources.

This book tackles these issues head on. It takes the reader on a fascinating journey from understanding how we think, and why we think the way we do, through to developing the radical positive behaviours required in today's workplaces, by developing skills in the new language of leadership.

This book is packed with useful ideas, insights, and models to guide and inspire everyone who works in individual, group or organisational settings.'

Eamonn Dunlea, Digital & Production Optimisation Partner, major Scandinavian dairy group.

'Well done...This is a deep, interesting and challenging read especially if you have some lean experience. It gets you thinking again!'
Prof. Dr. Richard Keegan, Adjunct Associate Professor of Lean Operations Excellence, Trinity Business School, Trinity College, Dublin.

'From someone who has read a lot of academic literature over the years, Deep Excellence *is by far the most intuitive book I have read: moreover, staying current in this research niche and field of organisational culture.* Deep Excellence *was crucial in helping me understand the link between head, heart and hands in a corporate results-based environment and where priorities must start for ideal results. A book truly committed to leading an enterprise on a journey to world class standards of Deep Excellence'.*

Elizabeth O'Callaghan, PhD Scholar, Bernal Institute, University of Limerick, Ireland.

What people say about this book.

'I think this book and the education/support offered by S.A. Partners has a very important role to play in helping businesses adjust their trajectory to deep excellence. The authors rightly point out that every situation is different. You may not have the right business ownership model, leadership talent or market conditions to go "full hog" from the start. Instead, you may have to adjust your approach to win a few Senior level hearts and minds with more traditional improvement impact (cost savings, capacity increase etc) before introducing the higher-level sustainability concepts discussed so well in this book. Nevertheless, this book delivers a rare view of "the dark side of the moon", a view which it's readers can use to guide their own journey to the stars. It may take time to achieve lift-off but without having the final destination in the navigation computer, it's quite likely you might end up on Venus!'

Simon Leonard, Global Director of Continuous Improvement, LGC Group

'Leaders now have a new moral obligation to eliminate waste and reduce resource usage in their organizations. This book provides an excellent practical guide on how to achieve this.'

Mike Larkin, Director People & Organisation Development Cork City Council

'Since the inception of the industrial revolution, the world and various industries have been transformed through the implementation of lean manufacturing tools and systems; however, the "sustainability" of those results are often challenged with the passage of time. There has to be another answer to the age-old question: How can we ensure sustainable results? Deep Excellence is that answer. Every leader needs to spend some time in this thoughtfully curated work to learn how to engage more of our ourselves - mind, heart and spirit! Then we will be armed with the ability to lead our teams, organizations and societies effectively through sustainable transformational change.'

Plant Manager, North American Automotive Company

Seeing and hearing a culture of

Deep Excellence

John Quirke

Juliette Packham

Simon Grogan

Bryan Cutliff

Deep Excellence

Seeing and hearing a culture of deep excellence

Published by S A Partners, Y Broth, 13 Beddau Way, Caerphilly, CF832AX, UK.

First Published 2023

A CIP catalogue record of this book can be obtained from the British Library.

ISBN: 978-1-9993748-4-6

The publishers have made every effort to trace and acknowledge copyright holders. If any source has been overlooked, we would be pleased to address this for future additions.

Cover illustration created by Alex Everitt.

About the authors

John Quirke originally graduated from the National University of Ireland Maynooth with an honour's degree in Chemistry and Biology. John subsequently completed a master's degree in chemical oceanography with University College Galway. A specialisation in metal chemistry led John to an early career as a chemical process engineer with Fujitsu Isotec, where he spent time in Japan studying Japanese manufacturing and engineering techniques. John's knowledge of process chemistry and toxicology resulted in a move to safety and environmental management with a blue-chip life science corporation. John's frustration with poor equipment design and poor process performance resulted in the early adoption of lean thinking within this organisation. The success of subsequent programmes, giving rise to improvements in process performance and waste reduction, led to global roles as director of business excellence and twenty-five years' continuous improvement experience working across all business sectors. In 2019 along with his colleagues Peter Willmott, and Andy Brunskill John published *TPM a Foundation of Operational Excellence*. The publication won the Shingo Institutes international publication research award in 2022. John is a senior partner at S A Partners and leads the Global Life Science and Health sector. John supports the development and publication of thought leadership within the business. John's other specialist areas include coaching and lean leadership, strategy deployment, process design for lean, and problem solving. John is a certified Shingo Institute Facilitator and a Master Lean Coach from Cardiff University. In addition to BSc (Hons) and MSc, John holds a Law Degree from University College Cork.

About the authors

Simon Grogan has dyspraxia, which means whilst being particularly bad at any sport that requires co-ordination, he is clumsy, falls over, gets lost a lot, can be frustrated easily and worst of all finds reading and writing very difficult. Growing up in the nineteen seventies Simon's dyspraxia was never diagnosed – he was treated as a kid who was just a bit thick. Out of sheer bloody mindedness Simon learnt to cope with his dyspraxia and managed to bundle his way through his education. Work has been much easier, systems, numbers, processes, deadlines all help, they provide structure and help him think. As his career progressed, Simon became successful occupying various senior management positions and winning various best factory awards. In the year two thousand, two crazy things happened in Simon's life: the first was the birth of his daughter Molly, and the second was joining S A Partners. Both have taught him so much about people and helped him try to bring the best version of himself to work each day. Today he is the Managing Director and Chairman of S A Partners. If someone told the embarrassed eight-year-old boy, as his teacher tore up his English homework in front of the class, that one day he would be a joint author of a book, he would never have believed them.

About the authors

Juliette Packham graduated from Coventry University with an honours degree in Industrial Product Design. After a short time as a Design Engineer, Juliette was appointed to a major Business Lean Transformation Project. Here she grew her Lean thinking skills in Operations, Logistics and Warehousing where she quickly realised that problems within these areas often stemmed from a poor approach to New Product Introduction. Observations in the lack of systemic thinking during this time also helped pique her interest in leadership behaviours and managing change. Juliette went on to head up an Engineering Department and spent time working on systemic transformation by integrating teams across the business to reduce lead times and improve connectivity. Since joining S A Partners in 2004, Juliette has built on her passion for Leadership Development and Culture Change and supports a wide range of companies in different sectors as both a consultant, coach and mentor. She is the Global People Director and a Partner within the business, a Master practitioner in SoundWave and VoicePrint, an EMCC accredited Senior Coach/Mentor and is working towards a Diploma in Behavioural Science. Her passion for New Product Development systems continues, and she also spends much of her time working in Strategy Deployment, Tier Management Systems and with Leaders working on Organisational Culture Change.

About the authors

Before joining S A Partners, Bryan served as a Chief Executive Officer in small to medium-sized businesses, specifically within the healthcare industry. During this time, he promoted the importance of creating value for customers, employees, and stakeholders by focusing business resources and efforts on enhancing organizational engagement. Bryan specializes in helping organizations to leverage their strategic vision and use communication models to improve the safety and quality of the services rendered, deliver an exceptional customer experience, deepen relationships with employees, and achieve operational objectives. Bryan's expertise also includes organizational assessment, leadership development, personal and team development and coaching, conflict management and resolution, business negotiations, program facilitation, and change management. Within these areas, Bryan has worked with front-line employees, regional and national executives to cascade the organization's purpose while improving the quality and safety metrics throughout enterprises in which he served. Bryan holds a Bachelor of Arts in Speech Communication from Utah State University, Master of Business Administration and Master of Science in Health Administration from The University of Alabama at Birmingham, and a Doctor of Psychology in Leadership Psychology from William James College.

Preface

'Seeing and Hearing a Culture of Deep Excellence'

There is so little that we really understand. This struck me one evening working late in my new home office. The COVID pandemic identified a critical constraint in my ability to step into the world of home working. Broad band access!

While I live in a beautiful part of the world, sadly access to high-speed broadband is limited and working from home was now a must do. I reviewed options and discovered that the top of our "Back Field" provided line of sight to a local 4G mobile tower which was hidden from our house by a coniferous forest across the valley.

Thus began our COVID lockdown project number one: home office. Various options were considered but we eventually opted for an upcycled shipping container which was already labelled, *'Cabin 36'*.

So here I was locking up from Cabin 36 and preparing for my walk down to the house below. As I turned off the lights my eyes adjusted to reveal a spectacular star scape. Taking the time to enjoy the view, I remembered a very humbling piece of information I had once read. Ninety five percent of what I was looking at is unknown to modern science. While I could see stars and galaxies, these account for only five percent of the known universe. Most of the vista stretched before me consisted of dark matter and dark energy of which we know almost nothing except for the fact that it is there.

So, what has this got to do with a book on organizational excellence? In a word, it is about humility. If the years 2020 and 2021 are to teach us anything it is humility as a race. We have seen how vulnerable our way of life is to disruption. While we have been successful in developing vaccines for this current challenge, there will be more. Other viruses lurk and are waiting for the opportunity to use humans as new hosts and vectors; global warming and the over-consumption of resources is a reality which is only just beginning to really tweak our consciousness.

So again, what has this got to do with a book on organizational excellence? There have been many efforts in the past to describe organizational excellence and how to make it sustainable and impactful. Success is often measured as individual's or organization's accumulation of value for its stakeholders. However, we see organizations achieve levels of success and excellence, yet they can still be incredibly wasteful in their use of physical resources and the precious time given to them by their employees.

It is time to change our thinking. It is time to consider what true sustainable organizational excellence could look like. It is time to think about levels of Deep Excellence.

By Deep Excellence we mean a pervading culture, with levels of communication and mutual respect, that allows an organization to perform at consistent and ever-improving levels of excellence across its entire network.

It is a culture based on transformative participation where everyone understands the need and actively participates in their organization's improvement. Individuals actively participate because they want to be part of the story and wish to see their small part, their legacy, in making that story a reality.

It is a culture that goes beyond an individual site. Accolades received at a specific site level, which may be justified, often do not represent the level of performance across the wider and larger corporation where its associated supply-chain performance remains poor.

Deep Excellence does not rely on the charisma of one leader. We often see the success or failure of a culture change initiative being dependent on an individual site leader. This leader 'gets it', and yet they often spend much of their organizational energy weaving through the unrealistic or poorly thought through efforts of 'Corporate' cultural and behavioural change programmes.

Deep Excellence is a social contract within and around an organization independent of any individual leader. Agreed standards of behaviour, improvement and real social consciousness intertwine seamlessly to deliver ever-improving levels of performance for the business, its staff and the planet itself.

Many of the concepts are simple. Yet the ways we currently measure what "good looks like" actively work against efforts to achieve Deep Excellence.

In this book we will be provocative and challenge current thinking. Because it needs to change.

> There are obvious problems in the way business functions work together and measure results.
>
> Despite all our learnings around quality and the science of process improvement most business activities are incredibly inefficient and wasteful.
>
> Systems and processes that are supposedly designed to achieve consistent high levels of quality, instead drive behaviours that deliver the opposite effect.
>
> There are mind boggling complications in how functions within organizations work together to achieve at best mediocre and often fleeting levels of good performance.
>
> Organizations talk of empathy with the current and future needs of its customers or patients, but it often lacks empathy with its own employees.
>
> Functional departments can often consistently ignore the needs (customer value) of other departments which are crucial to delivering overall value to the customer.

Organizations that move in the direction of Deep Excellence tend not to focus on *'Lean Tools'* or *'Improvement Projects'*. Instead, they focus on culture and behaviours. These are the agreed behaviours or *ways of working* they need expressed at given moments of time, in every aspect of their business, to ensure sustainable improvement.

> *How should our salespeople behave with a customer in a way that gives us the best chance of winning sustainable business?*

What would we see a machine operator do or say in the event of a process breakdown or quality concern that allows the business to react and learn from the issue in the best possible way?

What are the behaviours we need to see in our research and development teams to ensure we achieve the shortest 'Time to Break Even' when the product is introduced to the market?

When organizations take the time to really understand what these behaviors look and sound like, they begin to ask a very important question.

Do the systems and processes in our organization enable or disable the expression of these ideal behaviors?

So, take a breath, base yourself in a mindset of humility and empathy, and begin to explore what Deep Excellence can look and sound like in your organization.

We hope our thoughts captured in this book will act as a catalyst to drive real and meaningful discussions in your organization as to what Deep Excellence might look like for you.

So go and see the reality. Make it visible and strive for a meaningful, impactful, and sustainable level of excellence. You have the power to influence what is happening directly around you.

So, begin. Move your thinking and that of your organization's towards **Deep Excellence.**

Foreword by Rose Heathcote

Deep Excellence is a book about people, human nature, humanity and preparing for the future. Written in a thoughtful, unpretentious, and empathetic style, the authors usher the reader through a story of learning, challenging current mental models, provoking new ways of thinking and acting with purpose.

As I page through the book, I am enthused by the *Ubunti* spirit intertwining the chapters. *Ubuntu* is a word of African origin meaning *I am because we are* and *humanity towards others*. Ubuntu embraces the idea that we can only be human, together. That what we do as individuals affects the greater good. That the behaviours we live influence and affect those around us. This is an important theme which I believe we should all reflect on and propagate as we orient tribes through turbulent times toward a sustainable future.

We live and lead in exciting times. Leaders have always had to face disruption, volatility, uncertainty, and complexity but impending challenges bring unknown problems, calling for solutions not thought of before. Tugging on a growth mindset and transcending current learning thresholds. This is a call to action for a fresh kind of leadership delivering a new kind of value. With various forces at play and in constant flux, leader development is vital as customers, competitors, employees, investors, communities, and law makers toss organizations new balls to catch and juggle. But what does great in a leader look like?

The emergent leader, focused on solving issues of our time, values and develops people and is not compelled to lead by spreadsheets alone. This leader is willing to learn, adapt, empathise, and openly confess they cannot possibly hold all the answers. These leaders are bold, courageous and live the behaviours they wish to see in others. They have cool minds yet warm hearts. These leaders understand that all hearts, heads, and hands need to be on deck to solve those problems not identified before. For instance, as mitigation and adaption to climate change, protection of ecological boundaries, and development of stronger social foundations move into strategic pole position, building leadership resilience is exactly what a sustainable future relies on. Self-reflection, self-correction, self-leadership, self-empowerment, self-education—rewriting internal monologues, as the authors suggest, offering optimism and new pathways for success. These characteristics differentiate leaders of the future while loading them with personal, competitive advantages that bring employability rewards too.

In my 27 years of studying lean and, over the last decade, sustainability, I've come to appreciate the enormous task of linking strategy with what people are accomplishing daily at the gemba. As the authors advocate, performance is won or lost at the frontline, and this is where the vision (or lack thereof) manifests. This is where we witness strategy connecting with on-the-ground action, or not. And building people who solve problems, every day, that matter, is the golden access key. This is also the power of thinking lean—a way to unite the tribe, strengthened by diversity, to accomplish big things together. *Ubuntu*.

In the book you will find a clear banding of this big picture with what can be tried and tested on the ground, animated through the authors' choice of words, personal stories and guiding principles. Stories such as the farrier who cares for his horse's hooves while also connecting with his subject on a deeper level. Principles that foster a line of sight from what we set out to do to the behaviours that enable work to be accomplished in a better way. Themes to help the leader shift from a zone of comfort to a zone of learning and growth.

Experiences captured in the book draw from the consulting stage and serve not as a verbatim roadmap to follow heedlessly, but as inspiration for what is possible and what questions to ask. Toyota is not threatened when visitors and competitors walk their gemba in search of answers, because the answers to transformation do not lie only in what is visible but, in the underlying philosophy, principles and within the spirit of a company. The spirit of kaizen in Toyota is noticeable in their resilience to weather storms, augmented through their chosen behaviours. They openly share insights and learnings (as do the authors) which does not relinquish competitive intellectual property but makes it available to those willing to do the work and prepared to develop a deeper understanding. Every leader must walk their own path discovering the behaviours that will bring the right results, setting a new bar, by learning from those who have been there before.

We are reminded that tools, projects, technical knowledge are not enough to satisfy customers and catapult organizations to new levels of performance. Recognising the hard-wire our minds have suffered throughout our brain's history, we can now challenge dated beliefs and assumptions in search of a new way of thinking. Couple this with sincere commitment to people, and you have winning ingredients for excellence.

Deep Excellence appeals to leaders to lift themselves out of the detail of the functional silo into the world of systems and common vision, offering a prime view of the impact that can be accomplished when examined from these heights. Seeing the whole and scientifically seeking out root causes and leveraging system change. Aligning efforts from a systems perspective, considering interrelationships, challenging underlying assumptions while injecting a healthy dose of reality from the gemba. In this way the work at a deeper level is more focused and effective.

It's time to recognise that organizations and their connected systems are plagued more with process failures than people failures. Helping people remove barriers, problem by problem, setting up an environment for growth, success and innovation is far more productive than pointing fingers at guilty parties. Building such an environment that is stable and safer to work in, demonstrates respect for people and earns trust. A key tenet of thinking lean.

Leaders striving for excellence are urged to go deep, liberating themselves from comfort zones and stepping into optimal anxiety zones of learning and growth. This is an exciting time to stand out and make a real difference through people.

Yesterday I was clever, so I wanted to change the world.

Today I am wise, so I am changing myself.

- 13th century Persian poet, Rumi –

Rose Heathcote served as CEO for the Lean Institute Africa (Lean Global Network), CEO for Thinking People and Head of Sustainable Enterprise for the University of Buckingham.

Acknowledgements

As far as we know we have one life. For those of us who must work to earn a living, work takes up a major part of that life. I am grateful that I have worked with some tremendous groups of people in my life. Over the last fifteen years the team at S A Partners have been such a group.

I did not write this book, they did. The expertise, experiences and stories shared have all helped to develop me to a point where I am privileged to capture these joint experiences and learnings in this book. I am grateful for the time and space the team have given me to sit down and write.

Special thanks to Simon Grogan, Juliette Packham and Bryan Cutliff who took time out of their busy consulting schedules to put their thoughts and experiences down on paper.

Also, thanks to our clients – some of whom may recognize themselves in this book. I am always impressed by the openness of companies to share their experiences with those who are beginning their journey to sustained enterprise excellence. This is a powerful force for change and improvement which will be needed over the coming decades.

Finally, thanks to my family Zita, Julianne, and Eoin for their encouragement and patience. Consultancy is a tough gig! A lot of time is spent away from home. Adding book writing on top of a consulting schedule has been a challenge. I could not do what I do without their support.

From S A Partners

The Partners would like to thank John and his fellow authors, Bryan, Juliette and Simon for all the hard work and dedication that's gone in to producing this book on behalf of our business.

This book represents the evolution of our thinking as a consultancy over the past 30 years. We have learnt that sustainable success can only be achieved when the why, the how and the what are truly aligned. Organizational challenges are rarely solved by process fixes alone, invariably the real challenge lies within the people and how they are managed and lead.

This book helps us further understand how identifying organizational purpose together with defining the necessary systems, culture and behaviors are the essential first steps in any transformation journey. It also demonstrates how dynamic, flexible leadership can be created to deliver Sustainable Enterprise Excellence.

Contents

1 Our Evolutionary Legacy

1.1. Why leaders need to focus on culture behaviors.

The soft stuff is the hard stuff. This is a quote often attributed to Jack Welsh of GE. By soft stuff we mean the pervading culture and behaviors within an organization. But what do we even mean by that? It comes down to the behaviors we see and hear happening in the workplace day-to-day during 'normal' activities and in times of stress and crisis. Meetings, shop floor day-to-day interactions, conversations with customers, patients or clients all give opportunities for the true nature of organizational culture to 'seep out' and be expressed, allowing the true culture of the organization to become visible and audible.

These behaviors, driven by the mindset of the individual at the time, are something very real and have a direct consequence on business activity. A salesperson expressing frustration to the customer about the organization he or she works for is an expressed observable behaviour. A leader with little or no connection to the shop floor who tells a group of subordinates how to resolve a problem, is an expressed behaviour which will drive long-term less than ideal consequences within the organization. A supervisor or manager who ignores or accepts a breach in standards so as to avoid a difficult conversation is an expressed behaviour that can have critical far-reaching consequences.

On the other hand, a salesperson who speaks knowledgeably, and perhaps even lovingly, about the organizations they work for can build confidence with a potential customer. A leader who takes the time to listen, inquire effectively to understand, and then provides the appropriate coaching support creates an environment of trust, confidence and learning within a team. A supervisor who will immediately react constructively to a non-compliant situation and who will go deeper into the root cause behind that non-compliance is an immensely powerful asset to their team and the organization they work in.

So, what is it about culture and behaviour? Why is it so obvious and yet so hard? Why do so many publications, including this one, harp on about it so much?

The fact is that our brains are hardwired with "default settings" which lead us to behave in ways that are, by their nature, detrimental to achieving long-term sustainable excellence in our workplace. It is this level of pervading excellence in all aspects of the organization's activities that we refer to as deep excellence.

Leaders must be constantly aware of the evolutionary traits within all of us and their potential impacts on their own thinking and that of their teams. These traits - our combined evolutionary legacy - are an ever-present feature of our stone age brain.

1.2. Our modern skulls are home to a stone age mind.

Looking at the night sky we can get a sense of infinity and our place in the universe. But we often miss the brief length of time we as a species have spent on this planet as a rational self-reflective organism.

I love the time maps that compress the 4.5-billion-year history of our planet into one year. A familiar time stamp such as the extinction of the dinosaurs occurs on the 26th of December of that year. The first recognisable human beings appear at 11:35 pm on December 31st. Human language is estimated to have developed sixty thousand years ago, about seven minutes before midnight in our compressed year. The industrial revolution and all its consequential impacts on our planet occurred just **one half second** before midnight on the 31st of December in that compressed planetary calendar year.

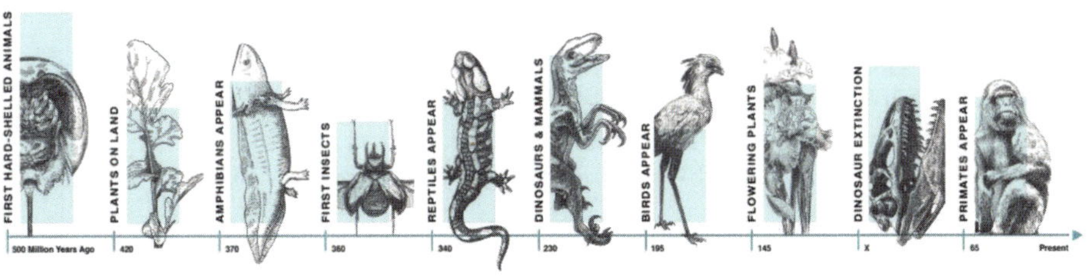

Figure 1: Our evolutionary Legacy. © S A Partners.

As a species, we now live in increasingly extensive communities which are impacting the way our planet works and sustains life. It is sometimes frightening to think that our species has this power and yet we are still driven by complex interactions between our neurons and hormones — with nervous and endocrine systems that have remained largely the same as those possessed by our stone age ancestors. Given our growing impact on our planet, driven by our industrial activities, I believe there is a need for a greater awareness of our innate prehistoric traits which often lead to suboptimal and highly wasteful business and team performance.

1.3. Evolutionary Psychology

The way our brain is structured and the behavioural instincts it supports works in the same way as the brain our ancestors Homo Sapiens used to solve problems and interact with their cultural units some 315,000 years ago. Evolutionary Psychology suggests that as our ancestors were faced with challenging situations their instinct and intelligence allowed them to survive and thrive, passing their DNA-based advantages to their offspring and eventually to us. But the reactions in our brain arise from mechanisms which go back much further than our hominid ancestors.

Evolutionary psychology is a growing area of study giving us a much deeper understanding of the complex nature of our brain, its neural pathways, its interactions with our hormonal system, and how these interactions have a direct impact on our state of mind and general feelings of wellbeing.

Evolutionary psychologists often refer to five basic principles that underlie their thinking:

> Your brain is a physical system that instructs you to behave in a manner appropriate and adaptive to your environment.
>
> Your mind (the way we think) is based on the adaptive changes that originated in the Pleistocene era which started 2.6 million years ago.
>
> Most of your psychological behaviors are determined subconsciously by your neural circuitry and we are largely unaware of these subconscious processes.
>
> The neural circuitry in your brain helps us solve problems in an appropriate manner. The specific ways that the neural circuitry is constructed are directed by natural selection over the course of generations.
>
> Neural circuits in the brain are specialised for specific functions.
>
> (Cosmides & Tooby, 1997)

In simple terms, while most of us no longer wander around the fields and jungles of Africa, many of us wander around the fields and jungles of the workplace with the same brain structures and instinctual responses of our early ancestors over three hundred thousand years ago.

Three hundred thousand years ago, knowing who's the 'boss', making friends, and keeping in with your nomadic tribe were important for survival. Without the protection and co-operation of the tribe survival would have been difficult, if not impossible. A quick response to a sense of danger, and the instinctive fight-or-flight reaction it precipitated, increased the likelihood that your genes would be passed on over those of your less reactive relatives.

Like it or not, this evolutionary legacy is hardwired into our brains. It can define how we interact with our close groups and how quickly we think about 'others' — those not like us, or different. It defines how we respond to challenges and stressful situations. Equally, it forms the basis of what feelings of trust, belonging, and even love mean for us, and how these feelings are triggered by very real hormonal release into our bodies.

1.4. The Structures of our brain

At a very basic level there are four areas of our brain that play a part in this story. The Brain Stem and its direct connection to the spinal cord is largely responsible for basic unconscious bodily functions. The Cerebellum is responsible for balance and co-ordination. The Limbic System triggers our emotional responses, and the Cerebral Cortex is associated with cognition, thinking, and problem solving.

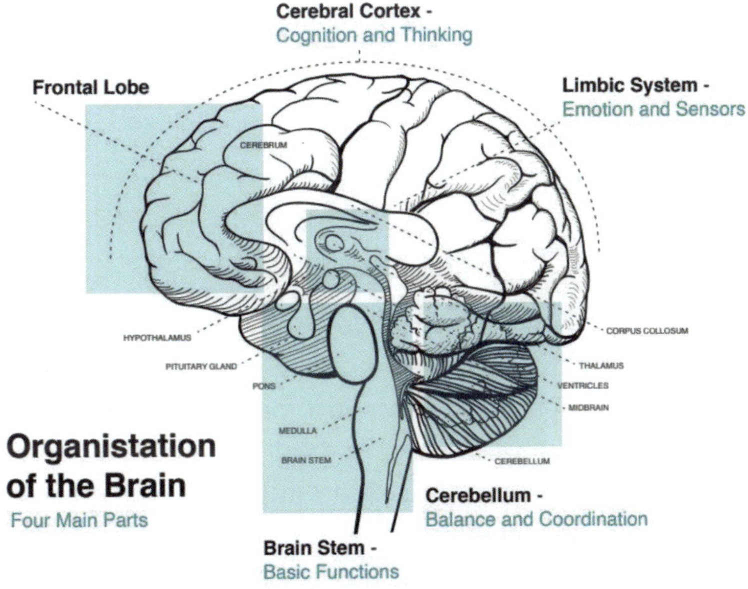

Figure 2: The structures of our modern brain are largely the same as our ancient tribal ancestors over 200,000 years ago. © S A Partners.

The cerebral cortex is the part of our brain where we are most 'human'. We can think logically and solve problems; we can understand and process information. Within the Limbic elements under the cerebral cortex, we experience joy, kinship, and feelings of being part of something bigger than ourselves. Here we can think and rationalise for the self.

However, we can move very quickly from our higher brain to the lower 'older' parts of our brain such as the amygdala—the "lizard" brain. Here we are closer to the instinctual parts of the brain where fight-or-flight and survival mode reactions are triggered. This region of the brain is where we process fear by stimulating various endocrine systems, which can trigger powerful chemicals like adrenaline that redirect blood flow away from higher brain functions towards our inner organs, such as our heart and lungs, and towards our big *'I'm out of here'* muscle groups. In this state of stress, we tend not to think rationally. In this state we have the potential to fall into deep-rooted responses in how we think, what we say, and what we do.

This evolutionary legacy has three very important impacts on organizational culture and behaviors:

1. The impact of the tribe.
2. Our perceptions of reality and ability to problem solve in complex situations.
3. The impact of prolonged exposure to stressful environments.

Leaders must constantly work both with and against our inbuilt evolutionary legacy to keep the mindset of their teams away from the potential negative impact of these inbuilt modes within our brain. While we explain these negative impacts in detail below, there are also some potential positive outcomes arising from these evolutionary legacies particular in harnessing the positive nature of "the tribe" working together for a common purpose. Harnessing the positive and minimizing the negative impacts of our evolutionary programming is the constant work of leadership if they wish to move the organization to levels of genuine deep excellence.

1.5. The impact of the tribe

Our thoughts and actions are easily swayed by the tribe. It is better to stay with the tribe than be out on our own waiting to be picked off by a lion! Our behaviour towards others is also influenced by the tribe. That suspicious person on the distant ridge could be one of the others, and a possible risk, or someone in our own tribe who had different views to the rest of the tribe and its leader.

We believe the impact of the "tribe" on our way of thinking is one of the most significant legacies passed on to us, and one which organizations must constantly work against to avoid poor cultural and business outcomes.

In our consulting practice I often show leadership teams three parallel lines of different lengths labelled A B and C, with B being the shortest line. I then ask them: which is the shortest line? At this point the team often look at me as if I have lost my mind. The CEO looks at the CFO with a quizzical look, meaning 'how much exactly are we paying for this?' Undeterred, I persist, asking which line is the shortest? Exasperated, they answer (often shout): B! Well done, I say, do you think you would ever answer differently? It is at this point, just before the connection is made with security, that I ask the team to watch a short video clip produced by a gentleman by the name of Solomon Asch.

Interestingly, on several occasions someone in the room has seen this clip before and understands the point being made but they have remained silent allowing the team to watch the video uninterrupted.

The Asch experiment, carried out in nineteen fifties, is, for me, one of the clearest demonstrations of why leadership teams need to be constantly tuned in to the powerful force that is organizational culture and its associated behaviors. In his experiments, Asch asked groups of between eight and ten college students to participate in a "visual perception" experiment. Only one person was the real subject; the remaining members of the experiment were actors asked to give the wrong answer approximately two thirds of the time. The answers were given aloud. The subject is either second from last or last to answer (Asch, Effects of group pressure on the modification and distortion of judgments, 1951), (Asch, Opinions and social pressure, 1955).

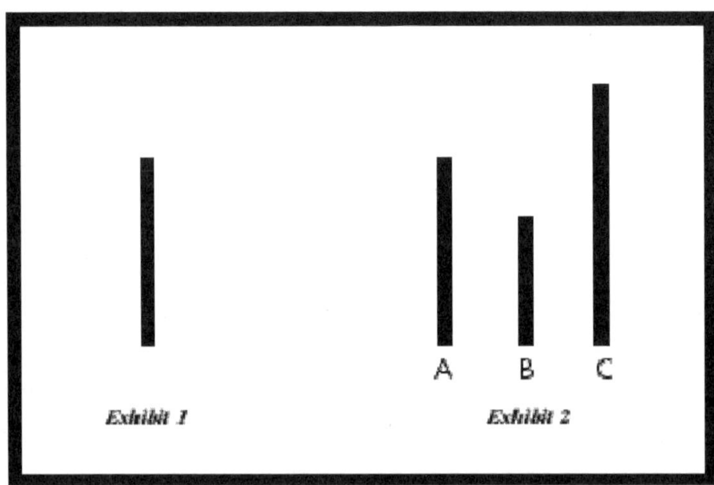

Figure 3: The Asch experiment (Asch, Effects of group pressure on the modification and distortion of judgments, 1951)

In the experiment individuals are swayed by the influence of the group to deny the simple evidence in front of them that the line labelled A is clearly the same length as the line on a card presented to the group. Yes, there were individuals who resisted the pressure from the group. However, the percentage of people who were influenced is very interesting.

Twenty-five percent of subjects were unaffected by hearing wrong answers. Seventy-five percent of subjects gave the wrong answer at least once. Of that group of seventy-five percent, thirty percent followed the tribe and gave wrong answers consistently.

Think of that number of people following the tribe without question. In follow-up interviews conforming individuals admitted doubting the answers of the majority of the group but followed the majority consensus anyway.

During the interview after the experiment the explanations given for participants' nonconformity included confidence in one's own judgment or the obligation to stick to their answers (Asch, 1955). While those conforming to the group gave explanations such as: "I am wrong, they are right," "not to spoil your results," or the idea that something was wrong with them for seeing the answer differently, so they wished to hide this (Asch, 1955).

'Even those who conformed believed that, perhaps, the members who gave wrong answers were seeing an optical illusion, yet they followed the majority anyway' (Asch, 1955).

There has been much criticism of the Asch Experiment and the conclusions drawn from it, but personal experience and wider information in relation to social media and its influence on thinking suggests that the influence of the tribe is very real. *(Ref Down the Rabbit hole our Stolen Focus).* In an organizational context, following the dominant 'tribal view' or the dominant culture can have positive or negative consequences on the sustainable success of that organization. As we will discuss later in this book, organizations need to ensure that systems and processes in the organization are designed and regularly reviewed to ensure that the dominant culture and expressed behaviors are those that will ensure the long-term success of the business rather than a cause of its failure.

1.6. Perception of reality and problem solving in complex environments

Another important legacy arising from the way our brains have evolved is it use of energy. Our brains are big lumps of hungry tissue. There is some debate as to why we have such big brains (reference). While they may give us the advantage of solving problems, they also require a lot of energy. Our brains take up around four percent of our body size but use twenty percent of the energy we consume. We are not going to discuss brain size and evolutionary advantages except to assume that the environment of our ancient ancestors was seldom stable. The ability to constantly rationalise situations, make strong social connections and solve new problems gave them an advantage on the evolutionary ladder, and so here we are. But this comes at the price of high energy consumption in that lump of tissue between our ears!

To overcome excessive energy demands our brain likes to take and make shortcuts, create habits, and save energy. Our vision and thought processes are designed to create high levels of focus when required, such as: '*there's that lion again!*' We have an incredible ability to concentrate but it comes at the loss of peripheral levels of consciousness. That is, we can easily miss stuff.

One of the best demonstrations of how we can miss stuff is uncovered by the fascinating work of Daniel Simons and Christopher Chabris and their studies of the limits of our attention (Simons & Chabris, 1999) (Simons D. J., 2000).

Their "invisible gorilla" test had volunteers watching a video with two groups of people: some dressed in white, some in black. The video shows the individuals passing basketballs between each other. The observers are set a clear task: count the passes among players dressed in white only, forcing the observers to ignore the passes of those in dressed in black T-shirts. Approximately fifty percent of the individuals who are engrossed in counting the passing of basketballs completely miss the fact that a large gorilla walks through the scene, faces the camera beats its chest and walks out of the frame. Seems incredible, but I must admit to being one of those people when I first saw this video nearly twenty years ago!

At the time, like many people, I could not believe it. I was convinced it was a con and that there were two videos. Nope, there was only one video. My brain like so many other people focused on the defined task at hand. I completely missed the big black hairy gorilla that walked straight into the shot. At the time I was very disappointed, but the experience did spark an incredible interest in how our brains work and how we truly perceive reality.

At the time I was first introduced to “the gorilla”, I was working in a blue-chip global organization. It was an interesting period for me and the organization in which I worked. The organization needed to change, and fast. I found myself as the person responsible for initiating and guiding a culture to radically change how that organization worked and constantly improve its work.

To begin the journey to our new self, as an organization and as members of teams within the organization, we needed to see the true reality of our performance and focus on radically improving it. Instead of getting stuck in the proverbial weeds, we engaged teams in *‘taking a step back’*, *‘drawing the big picture’* and asking annoying simple questions such as: *‘what are we actually trying to achieve here as a team?’* Very quickly we began to see our own gorillas, and lots of them.

Again and again, Simons and his colleagues have shown through experiments how easy it is for us to miss detail in the environment around us — which he has referred to as “inattentional blindness”. The Spot the Gorilla video has been in circulation since 1999, so it is difficult to find fresh “victims”. But Simons has built on the notoriety of the original video to prove the principle once again. I am not going to spoil the surprise for you so go and see the video yourself!

In a recent interview with Choi (Choi, 2011) of the website *Live Science* Simons explained:

> Although people do still try to rationalize why they missed the gorilla, it's hard to explain such a failure of awareness without confronting the possibility that we are aware of far less of our world than we think
>
> I thought it would be fun to see if I could monkey with people's intuitions again using almost the same task
> Simns, in (Choi, 2011).

Commenting on the results of his studies Simons noted:

> You can make two competing predictions. Knowing about the invisible gorilla might increase your chances of noticing other unexpected events because you know that the task tests whether people spot unexpected events. You might look for other events because you know that the experimenter is up to something. [Alternatively], knowing about the gorilla might lead viewers to look for gorillas exclusively, and when they find one, they might fail to notice anything else out of the ordinary.
>
> (Choi, 2011)

Despite viewers knowing what the new video is trying to do, Simons reported that only seventeen percent of those who were familiar with the old gorilla video noticed the unexpected events in the new video. In comparison, only twenty nine percent of those who had not seen the old video spotted the unexpected events in the new gorilla video. He noted:

> A lot of people seem to take the message of our original gorilla study to be that people don't pay enough attention to what is happening around them, and that by paying more attention and 'expecting the unexpected,' we will be able to notice anything important.
>
> [Simons added] *The new experiment shows that even when people know that they are doing a task in which an unexpected thing might happen, that doesn't suddenly help them notice other unexpected things.*
>
> (Choi, 2011) (My emphasis here).

Once people find evidence of the thing they're looking for,

> they often don't notice other things. (...) Our intuitions about what we will and won't notice are often mistaken’

Simons is quick to point out that the implications of his work not only relate to our visual senses but also impact the way we think, the way we remember and the way we reason: 'we think that everyone sees things the same way we do but this is far from the reality' Simons, in(Choi, 2011).

1.7. Inattentional blindness in our organizations

Now think about this from the standpoint of leaders trying to deploy a business strategy or supporting a team in how they deal with a problem. Or a salesperson meeting a customer or an instructor training a team in a new way of working. How aware are we of our own perceptions and how far does our view of the reality differ from the perceived reality of the person before us?

Unfortunately, our evolutionary brain structures leave us predisposed to miss things the more we focus on a task or are placed in stressful situations. That fact that we can be beset by "Gorillas" in our businesses, and our world view can be so very different from others, suggests that we should be relying on *more eyes and opinions* than our own.

However, to ensure such an open environment we need to be good listeners. Along with good listening skills we also need to actively create working environments in which individuals **know** that their opinions and ideas will be listened to and respected.

Unfortunately, many organizations fail dismally on both these fronts. Active listening, which includes keeping your mouth shut when you need to, tends not to be a skill we are born with or to which we owe credit to our ancient ancestors. Since we mastered the art of complex vocal communication, we seemed to have sacrificed the skill of listening!

Needing more eyes and voices than our own can often be compromised by the influence and power of 'tribal thinking' as mentioned earlier. To combat this, organizations need effective ways to nurture those brave souls who are prepared to point out that, no, in fact, the right line is line A!

1.8. The impact of stressful environments

Bookshelves are full describing the negative impact of stress on our overall wellbeing. Much of it attributed to our modern way of life. As mentioned earlier, we assume our ancestors faced stressful situations from time to time, but when we consider our population now to the human population 300,000 years ago, the struggle for resources may not have been as acute then as it is now! Our ancestors needed to engage the stress response mechanisms from time to time to survive. In our modern society we appear to be hitting the stress button all too often.

In general, we tend not to do well in environments where we are exposed to consistent and excessive levels of stress. Recent advances in neuroscience reveal how our brain is constantly changing and developing new pathways. This neuroplasticity is again something we can thank our early ancestors for. In effect it is how we learn. However, prolonged, and excessive levels of stress can have a major negative impact on the working of our brains.

The blood brain barrier normally protects the brain from many of the body's regulatory chemicals. Prolonged exposure to stress results in the weakening of this barrier allowing proteins responsible for inflammatory responses to impact on brain tissue and responses. Changes in ability to think rationally, problem solve, and the quality of our emotional social interactions are all negatively impacted by the incremental changes to our brain chemistry and function cause by excessive stress.

However, stress is a normal part of our daily lives and can be good for us. Stress can drive us to learn, improve and overcome challenges leading to greater self-appreciation and resilience. In a television interview the Welsh rugby Player Gareth Thomas described fear as a lazy emotion that takes away our energy. His recommendation to be brave and be excited, face up to and enjoy your challenges is echoed in the approach the Toyota Motor Company takes to its problems and challenges. Within Toyota problems and crisis are viewed as opportunities to learn even during the most challenging of situations (Liker & Ogden, 2011).

Provided an individual's training, questioning and diagnostic processes are adequate, stress can result in a rewarding environment for personal growth. In his book *Flow, The Psychology of Happiness* Mihaly Csikszentmihalyi describes how we grow as individuals within our stretch zone (Csikszentmihalyi, 2013).

As a leader, you need to understand your position on the learning graph, but also where you would position your individual reports and their teams. At Toyota stretch zone targets and measures that surround standards are built so that teams can push themselves and enable change and improvement.

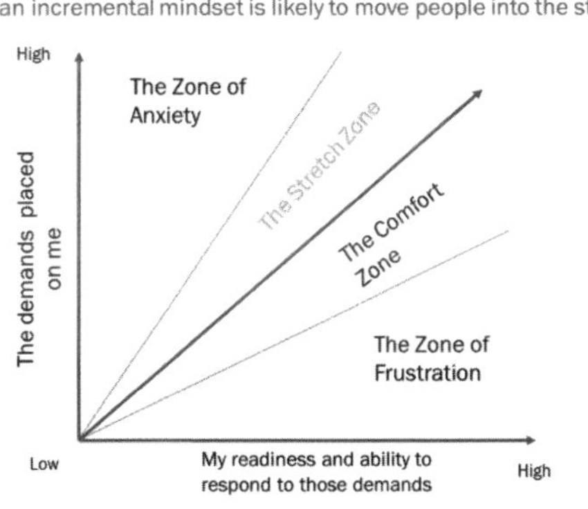

Figure 4: The Stretch zone of learning. (Csikszentmihalyi, 2013)

It is when the challenge we face is consistently beyond our competence and capacity that we can run into issues of mental and physical illness.

An organization that fails to recognise or appreciate the presence of destructive stress levels runs the risk of nurturing an underlying culture of fear. Fear can be one of the most sinister and destructive cultural forces in any organization. In his infamous publications of the mid-nineties Dr. W. Edwards Deming's 'System of Profound Knowledge' encouraged companies to drive out fear. A culture of fear reduces the likelihood of learning and growth. Accountability and ownership will be poor. Poor standards go unchallenged, errors are passed, and defects occur (Deming W. E., 1994).

1.9. Gaining control

Later in this book we will review how leaders can develop both their listening and communication skills and apply these effectively within structured work activity and casual opportunistic situations or "coaching moments". We will explain the many situations where the ability of the leader to listen and talk skilfully can have significant impact on the state of mind and therefore the expressed behaviors of individuals in an organization. We will describe how, through a consistent focus on the conscious development of effective listening, dialogue, and coaching skills, it is possible to radically change the culture and performance of an organization.

The move to more skilful interactions with teams becomes much more powerful if they take place with clearly defined systems within the business. By systems we are not referring to IT systems. Instead, we look at systems such as how we communicate within and outside our organization, how we improve all aspects of our business, how we ensure alignment to business strategy, how we make stuff and provide value. How we hire train and develop our people and how we capture our teams' valuable ideas and constantly improve the way work works in our organization.

Once we clarify these systems, we need to clarify the core aim of the system. We question: is the system driving the necessary focus and behaviors? Are there mechanisms within the system to ensure that we periodically take a step back and give ourselves the chance to spot our gorillas.

To begin our review of systems and the culture and behaviors they must support we must begin by getting absolute clarity on what it is you do in your business. The essence of the work that you do.

2 The essence of what we do

2.1. The essence of what we do

Few, if any, businesses feel they are in a stable business environment. There are always pressures to grow, change and improve. Some of these pressures may arise from external sources, while others are self-imposed. Either way the journey to levels of deep excellence is seldom direct or smooth.

It is important for organizations to truly grasp where they are on their journey to excellence. As a crude but powerful measuring stick, the graph below, the infamous 'squiggly line' as we refer to it - gives companies a reality check of where they are. Being open and honest about the reality of the current state is often a first step in harnessing the power of the tribe to move to a better place. In our consulting practice we often observe islands of excellence within organizations. This level of performance is down to an individual leader and the impact of that leadership on the performance of the team. Unfortunately, this level of excellence is not representative of the entire organization. Instead, this isolated island is diluted into a sea of mediocracy mediocrity where overall level of performance is far from optimal. Deep Excellence is also wide! There are no islands. Only an organizational wide focus to improve the efficiency and effectiveness of the entire value stream.

To effectively move along the squiggly line each element of the organization will need their own conversations and their own realization of where they are on the journey. Is the business in the red zone of unpredictability, high variations in performance and constant firefighting? Is the business in the yellow zone, in control and stable, but stagnant? Or are we really thriving building from one improvement to the next? From one newly created opportunity to the next? All driven by highly engaged and focused teams who understand customer value and the role they play in delivering and improving on that value offering.

Unfortunately, in many cases such a simple *'where are we now?'* exercise has not taken place. There is no looking forward, only managing the chaos of today: life in the red zone. In some cases, efforts at corporate benchmarking activity are often seen as a means of showing off rather than learning. Or hiding rather than revealing: a chore that must be done and then we get back to the day job.

To open a valid conversation around culture and behaviors a business must grasp the reality of where it is now. In later chapters we emphasize the importance of organizations completing a current state 'reality check' or maturity assessment as a first step on their journey to deep excellence. It will be impossible to drive for excellence with unclear or unstable systems of work. If we remain in the plateau, chances are we will slip back and decline. From the stability of the plateau, we must weave new stories and find new energies to continue to move towards sustainable levels of deep excellence.

Each zone of the journey requires different conversations around the behaviors and culture that will progressively move the organization from one zone to the next. The behaviors and culture to move from left to right are cumulative. The necessary behaviors focusing on standards, process design and accountability required to move from the reactive zone will not go away when we are in the proactive green zone, but here they become the foundation of the cultural fabric of how the business is run.

In moving from proactive to excellence, new behaviors and conversations will be required to avoid stagnation and regression. These behaviors are founded in the stretch zone of learning. They include constant curiosity and focus on the detail of process, the accumulation of marginal gains, and the excitement of breakthrough thinking, all observable behaviors that reflect a true learning organization. Teams have the time and resources to build deep and close relationships with customers and their current and future needs. These are the behaviors that help challenge teams to move closer to the ever-expanding world of deep excellence.

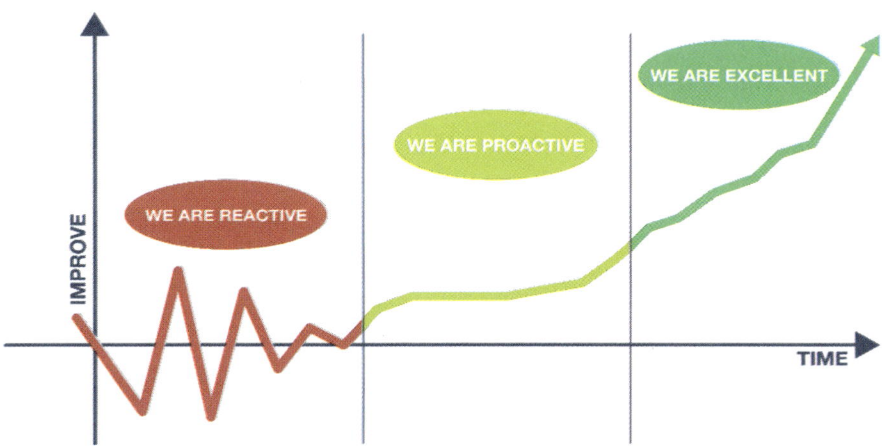

Figure 5: S A Partners 'Squiggly Line' and the phases of a journey to Enterprise Excellence. © S A Partners.

2.2. *Transformative Participation and Deep Excellence*

The ideal scenario to allow organizations to cope with the ever-changing business landscape (along with the drive to constantly challenge and improve on the status quo) is the need to develop a genuine deep-rooted culture of transformative participation. We spoke in the previous chapter of the paralyzing impact of fear in an organization. We also spoke of the impact of a telling culture, whereby a culture of dependency is created as teams wait to be told what to do. Developing a culture of transformative participation in an organization drives a completely new level of expectation around engagement and the value an individual derives from their work. The term *transformative participation* has been used in recent years in reference to the need to actively involve and engage minority groups in the design and implementation of legislative reform to protect vulnerable habitats around the world.

To engage these indigenous groups their real needs and day-to-day interactions with their environment must be clearly understood. Their voices and contributions must be included in any proposed changes to how a habitat is managed and protected. Transformative participation has also become a key element of linking disinterested public in the political mechanisms that influence their lives or to engage younger generations in national policy and environmental justice (Tisdall, 2013), (Coolsaet, 2015).

In the business of today there are many groups who are often excluded from decisions and changes that directly relate to the way they work. There can be many reasons given for this. Compliance considerations, insufficient knowledge and skills, not enough time to seek and analyze inputs, union considerations. Often this reasoning falls into a subtle policy where token engagement is sought which has little impact on the outcome. If this continues, teams rapidly become disengaged with an obvious impact on business performance.

Creating the expectation that transformative participation must exist across the organization sets a base level cultural expectation. It galvanises the fact that every individual has a role to play in contributing to and improving the work, the work environment, and how the organization contributes to the communities in which it operates.

> I measure success by the light in their eyes. When you see that spirit through the eyes and that spirit is dynamic, vibrant and on fire...what else do you need to know?

Thomas Hartman. Director of Operations Autoliv. Shingo prize winning facility. Shingo Institute Discover Excellence Training

Transformative participation is the active manifestation of deep excellence. It creates a cultural expectation on those who join the business and those who work, manage, and lead the business. It is the expression of a culture of continual improvement. A relentless call to action to make tomorrow better than today in all aspects of the way work is executed, resources consumed, and goals achieved.

2.3. *The cultural gap*

So why do we so often see a disconnection between desired culture and actual business performance?

Unfortunately, in many organizations, the values, behaviors and culture aspired to are not aligned to the way in which the business operates.

Take for example a health care setting: respect and dignity are often referred to as organizational core values. But what do these values mean in practice? How often do we see them ignored? Blocked up emergency departments, long waiting lists, and postponed procedures are all manifestations of a reality that is totally at odds with stated core values.

At a basic level, values of dignity and respect could mean staff listen to and understand patients' needs at every stage of the patient care pathway. These values could confirm staff are constantly aware of patient's privacy and ensure that dignity of the patient is taken into consideration at each treatment step, in the way they are prepared for their treatment and spoken to in relation to their treatment.

Sadly, in practice these aspired-for values are almost impossible to fulfil. Time-pressed and under-resourced staffing levels result in brief superficial interactions with patients at best. Pressure on costs results in the recruitment of agency staff whose first language may not match that of the majority of patients in care, resulting in poor and frustrating communication. The physical facilities within the environment may not facilitate the best efforts of staff to ensure the dignity of patients as regards the private communication of personal information and patients' personal physical privacy.

In these not-ideal circumstances, the expression of values is often left on the shoulders of individual members of staff. Individual nurses or managers try their best, give time to the patient, listen to them, argue for the patient's needs; but all too often these individuals who want to do the right thing give up, burn out or leave the organization.

Recognizing the disconnection of organizational values from the reality of day-to-day operations is often the first step on a truly sustainable journey to deep excellence.

2.4. Leaders and culture

The role of leaders in sustaining and developing the cultural basis for transformative participation cannot be overstated. Unfortunately, many leaders fail to reinforce desired behaviors through a lack of awareness or their adoption of a dominant but not ideal behavior within the organization. Often, they lack the appropriate skills to influence individual or group behaviors. More often, it is a combination of the above.

In addition, key systems within the business (the way work and activity is designed and managed) actively work against the expression of desired behaviors and culture.

In this chapter we will speak to the development of leaders' skills to influence behaviors to positively effect a culture of improvement. Chapter six will focus on the systems element to enable a culture of deep excellence.

2.5. Finding a real purpose?

When the age-old discussion around culture, values, and behaviors begins, one of the first questions leadership teams need to ask themselves is: why bother?

What should drive us to really consider culture and behaviors other than the sage voice of Peter Drucker echoing in our ears: '*Culture eats strategy for breakfast!*' We often gain comfort by looking at our results over the last few years and think...

'You know what? We're doing okay. We have ups and downs but in general, we hit our targets without all this focus on culture and behaviors.'

In our consulting practice we come across this thinking all too often. But the question should be, how is the organization achieving these 'okay' results? How much effort has it taken us? Could we have made it easier to get these results and maybe even better results?

Another version we see is 'The Corporate Programme'. The 'Corporation' have decided what our values and behaviors need to be. We (the site) have a timeline to communicate them and explain them to our teams. As a site we also have a timeline (usually short) to incorporate these new values into individual's personal development plans and annual reviews. These new values and behaviors have been developed by cross-functional focus groups in some part of the world. Where there is a need for local translations, the team have insured the 'values & behaviors' have the appropriate 'localization' context to aid interpretation.

Hands up, how many people have seen those programmes really work? Or how many people have embarked on such a programme only to find that the 'core values' change when a new leader is in the seat? Sure, they generate plenty of bum bags, pens, tee shirts and a variety of other landfill packers, but these efforts have little lasting impact. The local culture and behavior at a given manufacturing facility or shared service centre generally remains the same. It may even become a little more jaundiced as, yet another cultural change initiative fades into the wallpaper.

These situations are hugely frustrating for local leadership teams and can results in an erosion of trust in any focus on values and behaviors. Often leading to *'Here we go again'* dialogues within front line teams.

2.6. Getting to a genuine why?

When we begin to discuss values, beliefs, and behaviors within organizations, we often forget that we are in effect trying to 'get inside' people's heads and hearts! Personally speaking, my head tends to be a very important space for me! I have values that either motivate or demotivate me. To be my full self, ideally, I need to align my environment and social circle to my own beliefs and values. If I meet individuals or organizations that clash with my core values and beliefs, I can sometimes get involved in stimulating conversations where I can learn and expand or modify my value and belief system. However, where there is fundamental core misalignment, I tend not to spend too much time in that space. I might be able to tolerate the situation for a while but generally not for long!

In a very fundamental way, seeking the genuine why is an effort to link back into that ancient brain of ours. We are looking for that heartfelt tribal calling. A meaning to which we can apply our effort. A reason to contribute to a cause that is valued. It forms the basis for a culture of participative transformation.

The focus on participative transformation gives us a very different approach to thinking about behaviors and culture which must start at a site level. By site I mean the office, real or virtual, that we go to. The factory where we work together to make, cars, drugs, ready meals or garments. It is the hospital or educational establishment where we cure and educate people. These individual sites may be part of wider corporate organizations, but it is the actual expressed culture and behaviors within that individual site that count.

Many of the values expressed at corporate level may echo true within the site, however, the day-to-day, week to week performance of the site is dependent on the values and expressed behaviors required *at that site*. These are the actions we can see and the conversations we can hear within the teams that are necessary to ensure the consistent and efficient delivery of value to that site's customers. When they are aligned and working well, these ideal expressed behaviors are participative transformation in action.

2.7. *What could better look like?*

Let's go back to the *'why bother'* conversation mentioned earlier. Sometimes the need to think about culture change is clear. The site is not performing, there are behavioral issues and people in general are not happy. Engagement surveys are poor and employee turnover is high and overall labor costs are increasing.

While the need for change is clear in the scenarios above, we are often faced with this challenge from site leadership teams questioning the need for a culture change programme: The site has been doing fine, meeting targets and delivering what they need to deliver, and in fact saved $x million each year doing so.

When we meet leadership teams to discuss behaviors for the first time it can be a challenge. You can often cut the scepticism in the air with a spoon never mind a sharp knife! So, we often begin with a useful thought experiment. We encourage the team to focus on this next question.

We begin to explore the current level of performance. We ask questions about consistency of performance. We examine the current problems and issues and spend a lot of time with the team on the 'shop floor' in whatever form that takes. Once, we have a clear picture of the current state we ask the leadership team to participate in a thought experiment which we call the "magic wand moment". We ask the team the question.

> *Given what we now understand as the true picture of performance at the site – the problems, miscommunications, errors, and rework; the missed sales, failed or slow new product introduction, compliance issues etc. – we ask the leadership team to imagine they can 'wave a magic wand' and all the issues, the frustrations, errors etc are suddenly gone; how much better would things be?*

We allow the team to think in silence. We ask individuals to write down the "highly scientific" measure of *"betterness"* on a sheet of paper in terms of percentage. Ten Percent? Forty percent? What number would they put on the potential *"betterness"*? No peeking!

The team are then asked to present their thoughts on how much better things would be. After the magic wand was waved!

It is a bit of fun but with a serious edge. Seldom do we get a number that is less than sixty percent! Sometimes we get numbers of greater than one hundred percent! Yes, the site may be meeting its numbers and customer delivery targets, but the issue soon becomes a measure of the effort necessary to consistently meet and improve on these numbers. Or a realisation of the level of compliance risk which underlies the current level of performance which must be managed constantly.

Whatever the final percentage number is, if the leadership team can agree that there is a very real opportunity for "betterness", then they own the journey to get better.

Based on the challenges businesses and society in general will face in the coming decades, there is, I believe, a moral obligation on leadership teams to ensure they are getting the best outcomes from the people and resources they have at their disposal. Markets, legislation and customers will soon drive a new kind of business. Wasteful systems and processes that give rise to poor unreliable products and services will be challenged.

Given the agreed current state reality and this new obligation for optimal use of resources, it does not take much to open out the discussions to consider the behaviors that may be stopping the site achieving its true potential. Examples put forward can include observations such as...

> The way teams can behave in silos and fail to share important information at the right time.
>
> The way we create complexity to ensure compliance.
>
> The way we intentionally or unintentionally reward firefighting instead of doggedly pursuing root cause and eliminating potential issues before they occur.
>
> The way we consistently seem to repeat the same mistakes. As an organization we just don't seem to learn.

The fact that people team are reluctant to put up their hand if there is an issue.

Lack of accountability between key departments such as operations and maintenance.

Sales teams sell what they can sell rather than what the business needs them to sell.

We constantly blame external influences, and our teams behave like powerless victims waiting to be told what they can or can't do.

We don't communicate enough so expensive mistakes and misalignments occur and re occur.

We are not prioritising the critical issues!

With the right group this can be a real moment of change. The leadership team begin to see the day-to-day behaviors that hinder consistent excellence. If the atmosphere in the room is right the team often reflect on their own behaviors and the way in which they work together as a team.

We encourage the team to reflect on the impact their individual and collective behaviors have on the site. For example, if they do not hold each other accountable how can they expect to see this behavior consistently within the wider organization? If they feel the need to consistently jump into help solve problems how can the team learn about the process and solve problems for themselves? Are the priorities within the leadership team clear? This is very much a site-based conversation. While corporate values may act as a guide or framework, they tend to be at too high a level for the individual site.

So how do we begin to have real value-added conversations around the culture and behaviors needed at an individual organizational group? How do we align them to wider corporate structures? How do we make our conversations around the culture and behavior in an organization a fundamental element of our efforts at participative transformation towards Deep Excellence?

To begin to answer these questions we need to ask a very basic and frustrating question. What is at the core of our ability to deliver value? Or putting it another way what is the essence of what you do as an organization? As mentioned in earlier chapters there is often a deep disconnect between sought after values and culture and the tasks and activities that the majority of people in the organization actually do on a day-to-day, week-to-week basis. To move towards Deep Excellence, we must make a direct and purposeful connection between the value we create for our customers and the necessary behavior and culture within the teams to meet our 'value proposition' and constantly improve the team's ability to deliver on it.

2.8. Getting to the core

Our ability to deliver consistent value to our customers is dependent on one or two core elements of the way in which we do 'our work' and the real culture and resulting observable behaviors which support that work.

So how do we begin to have real value-added conversations around the culture and behaviors needed at an individual organizational team level? How do we align them to wider corporate structures? To begin to answer these questions we need to ask a very basic and frustrating question:

What is at the core of our ability to deliver value?

Or putting it another way.

What is the essence of what you do as an organization?

Our ability to deliver consistent value to our customers is dependent on one or two core elements of the way in which we do 'our work'.

At one stage in my life, I spent a lot of time caring for and riding horses. If you ever get the chance to see a farrier at work, take the time to observe the details of this ancient work system.

Figure 6: The ancient craft of a farrier.

The core of a farrier's ability to deliver value is to secure the right size and shape shoe to a horse's hoof. Once the skills associated with a farrier's work are grasped some of the most crucial behaviors behind the ability to do the work are calmness and safety.

A good farrier carefully picks the location where the horse will be shod. No risks of being trapped. No risk to the animal or the farrier. The farrier spends time stroking and sometimes nuzzling the animal soothing and calming it. The arrangement and sequence of tools in what is often a uniquely made toolbox are laid out to ensure the flow of work is smooth with no sudden changes and minimal noises. Can you see how the horseshoe nails are presented to the farrier in the picture above? All tools are in the exact place needed to ensure a smooth calm process while all the time the farrier calms and 'speaks' to the horse. When the work is finished, he again rubs and strokes the animal – building trust. They will see each other again soon.

But other behaviors are also important from a customer's perspective. Has the farrier arrived at the agreed time? I may have brought the horse in from a far field to have the animal ready and prepared for the farrier. As a customer it can be a pain if I am waiting around for the farrier to turn up! Is the work carried out in a reasonable length of time? 'A little less talk and a bit more action' can often apply!

On occasion a farrier has pointed out a health concern with the animal. Maybe an infection in the frog of the hoof. Or a swelling on the hock. The farrier may spot the issue and advise that a vet should look at the issue before it gets any worse.

These behaviors are very real; they link directly to the work that the farrier carries out every day. The expression of these behaviors make the difference between a *'must be tolerated'*, *'good'* and *'excellent'* farrier!

The behaviors we look for must be aligned to the work that we do.

2.9. Describing your essence.

'You need to figure out the behaviors that drive success in your organization…and recognize the heck out of them'

David Novak. Former Chairman & CEO Yum Foods. Author of Taking People with You.

So, what is at the essence of the way your organization provides value to your customers? In the following section we include some thoughts on observable behaviors within certain industry sectors. Please note that these are not defined lists. They are the accumulation of our own observations from the team at S A Partners during our consulting practice. The purpose is to provide some examples of very real positive and negative behaviors that we have observed.

If you try this exercise with your teams, you will need to create a safe space where teams can openly speak to and list the not ideal behaviors they experience which create frustration and make their work harder to do. It is very important that the discussions do not become personal, they should be kept at process level by looking at the consequential impact that negative behaviors have on process effectiveness or information flow.

> Q 'What makes it difficult to produce the important financial status reports on time?'
>
> A 'We don't get all the information we need at the right time'
>
> Q 'Is this a problem in all areas?'
>
> A 'No, some departments are better than others.'
>
> Q 'What is the business impact?'
>
> A 'The issuing of invoices is delayed resulting in cash flow issues for the business'

The conversation can then move to the impact on the business from not having the relevant information available at the right time. We do not focus on what person in what department. There may be issues in that department that we need to review, but the base behavior once agreed is the prompt delivery of the necessary information which is accurate and presented in the agreed format.

So, consider your own work environments, what is the essence of the work of your teams? Is the essence related to the need for detailed operational monitoring of large pieces of capital equipment as in energy generation or bulk chemical manufacture?

Figure 7: In a capital equipment intensive business. What behaviors are important?

POSITIVE BEHAVIORS	NOT IDEAL BEHAVIORS
Respect for Equipment – taking responsibility for workplace and equipment	Demarcation or silo mentality between support functions
Safety – active risk identification, control and communication	Poor or intermittent review and enforcement of work standards
Sharing observations on equipment performance to help improvement activity	Reluctance to share ideas
Problem resolution driven by curiosity and learning	Finger pointing and blame
Leaders present in work areas regularly supporting process performance improvement activity	Leaders focused on output figures
Co-development and ownership of work methods and performance standards	Little input from frontline on process design development

Leaders promoting and living safety and improvement activity	Work standards developed and reviewed by functional groups
Active and visible cooperation between functional and operational department	No ownership or accountability for workplace housekeeping or basic machine maintenance/cleaning
Equipment operators' opinions sought and valued in relation to equipment, performance improvement and new equipment purchase	Leaders seldom seen in work areas. No time given for improvement activity
Energy and waste consciousness.	Little effort at recognizing positive contributions

Is the essence of work based on care and compassion for those in care?

Figure 8: In a healthcare environment. What behaviors are important in this setting?

POSITIVE BEHAVIORS	NOT IDEAL BEHAVIORS
Respect for work environment – hygiene cleanliness, infection control	Demarcation or silo mentality between functions
Safety – active risk identification, control and communication between patients and colleagues	Gossiping/undermining colleagues
Active participation in hand over briefings being prepared and 'Present'	Criticizing process rather than support for improvement.
Supporting colleagues checking in regularly	Failure to follow-up, patient requests, information requests
Respect for dignity of patient and their family	Reluctance to engage with skill development and process improvement
Respect for patient confidentiality	Talking over patient
Listening to and seeking input from colleagues	Token or inconsistent approach to process standards
Awareness and respect for all colleagues involved in the patient care journey	Disrespect for colleagues and their contribution to patient care
Continual learning and self-development	Talking to rather than listening to patient

Is it the assembly of the intricate parts of a medical device or pacemaker?

Figure 9: Medical Device Assembly Line. What behaviors are important in this workplace?

POSITIVE BEHAVIORS	NOT IDEAL BEHAVIORS
Respect for Equipment – taking responsibility for workplace layout and equipment	Poor ownership or accountability for workplace housekeeping or basic machine maintenance/cleaning
Safety – active risk identification, control and communication	Poor or intermittent review and enforcement of work standards
Awareness and interest in upstream and downstream processes	Problem investigation improvement activity carried out by 'elite' groups with limited engagement with frontline teams
Understanding product use and patient impact ready to highlight any potential risks to product quality or compliance	Compliance culture resulting in over complexity and change paralysis
Flexible and willing to learn new skills	Reluctance to share ideas, fear of change
Strict adherence to current process standard while looking for opportunities to improve standards	Finger pointing and blame
Leaders present in work areas regularly supporting process performance improvement activity	Leaders focused on output figures
Co-development and ownership of work methods and performance standards	Little input from frontline on process design development

Leaders promoting and living safety and improvement activity	Work standards developed and reviewed by functional groups
All leaders reinforce positive behaviour and culture through effective recognition	Leaders seldom seen in work areas. No time given for improvement activity

2.10. Behaviors often extend beyond

Are your essential behaviors based on the need for close relationships with external third-party suppliers? There are many businesses today who rely totally on external suppliers for their product and service delivery. In some cases, there may be some internally controlled manufacturing or service activity, but the external value-adding element can be far larger. In these instances, it can be surprising to see the focus of management control and improvement activity is skewed towards the remaining internal processes. This is obviously a big miss for these organizations.

In one situation I spoke to an employee of a large pharmaceutical company whose role it was to review the quality of manufacturing and supply of a key raw material at an external manufacturer's site. The raw material in question represented a very small volume to the third-party suppliers' production volume and was not a key focus for them.

In speaking to the employee of their experiences of visiting the site they described the lack of interest and effort on the part of the supplier; in some cases the supplier was evasive and obstructive. Unfortunately, this was the case with several similar suppliers. However, the biggest and most disheartening issue affecting the employee was the feeling that they were alone in these difficult situations. They did not feel the support of their managers. For them, the lack of support and engagement in their feedback reports describing the behavior and attitude of the supplier was crushing. For the employee it meant that all this effort was for nothing. It was a tick the box exercise. Once the visit was completed it ticked the box. Solving issues arising from the visit was a whole different matter.

There were obvious risks in this situation, but the company seemed very slow to address them. There were other more pressing issues, but here lay a real risk that a supplier may not have the attitude or systems in place to ensure consistent delivery of quality raw materials.

This was an interesting situation. When challenged on the issues the leaders explained that they could not be responsible for the behaviors and culture in an external organization. However, following discussions it became clear that while they could not be responsible for culture and behaviors at an external manufacturer's site, they could create expectations of the type of culture and behaviors they would expect to be there.

In addition, it was accepted that the leaders were one hundred percent responsible for the culture and behaviors within their own organization. The fact that one of their employees felt alone and unsupported while visiting a 'difficult' supplier was their issue. They needed to find ways to ensure the process of external manufacturing site review had a very real and positive impact on the reliability of product supply.

The result was a more thorough risk assessment across the supplier network. Those identified as high risk or difficult were never visited by a sole employee. There would always be two reviewers and in critical instances one of these would be a senior leader. In addition, greater attention was paid to the finding of alternative suppliers for single sourced raw materials.

Given the situation described above, what are the good and not so good behaviors you could see or imagine within a group managing a network of external suppliers. Maybe there are examples in your own organization. Have a go. We have filled in a few.

Figure 10: External Supplier management.

POSITIVE BEHAVIORS	NOT IDEAL BEHAVIORS
Preparation and research prior to site visit	Being blinkered and avoiding issues that may 'make too much work' or be too hard to resolve'
Being familiar with product and process and compliance standards involved and regularly updated understanding and knowledge	Being disrespectful to staff and employees at the supplier's premises
Pre visit review and coaching by the reviewer's direct manager	Asking for repeated or non-value-adding information from suppliers

Are the essential behaviors you need based on the deep understanding of customer needs so that they can be translated into a marketing campaign or a new product design?

Think about this situation and consider potential positive and negative behavior that would directly affect outcomes for such a business. Would detailed quality research on the customer before any visit or contact be an example of a good behavior?

Figure 10: Understanding customer needs. What behaviors are important here? You have a go!

POSITIVE BEHAVIORS	NOT IDEAL BEHAVIORS

Are the essential behaviors you need based on constant creativity within your organization yet under fixed deadlines to meet advertising or production timelines and schedules? Would communication between teams and clear visualisation of project status be examples of useful behavior? What about how employees might carve out 'inspiration time' where they seek out creative environments to keep their own ideas fresh and current?

Figure 11: Creative design organization. What behaviors are important here? You have a go!

POSITIVE BEHAVIORS	NOT IDEAL BEHAVIORS

2.11. What behaviors for your organization?

In each case, if they are similar to your situation as an organization, or a local site leadership team, are you clear on the behavior you need to observe consistently to ensure your organization succeeds in delivering the essence of what you do?

It could be that your business requires a combination of things in different parts of the business. But what is at the real essence of how your organization brings value to your customers?

Companies can often get into a fair muddle trying to figure out what this is, but here is a hint: it tends to be what most people actually do in your organization!

What? What about the importance of our new product development team, or the sales teams, or how finance works or or or...?

But let's tease that out. Let's say we are a medical device assembly operation making complex medical devices. The reliability and performance of the process is slightly above average with a tendency to wobble but generally retains a good level of performance.

How good do you think the introduction of new products to that process will be?

How accurate will the financial information relating to the true performance of the process be?

How confident might the salesperson feel when she is in the field taking orders and managing demand?

Contrast the above to a situation where the process is performing at consistently high levels. In this organization we can see trends to show how that performance continues to improve. We see levels of incredible detail around process design and standardisation. We see examples of learning and ideas for improvement from all members associated with the process. Now ask the three questions above again. How different will the answers be?

2.12. Pulling it together

To move an organization on a path to truly sustainable deep excellence there must be a reckoning on the true reality of where the organization as a site is now. There must be a very real conversation around the essence of what the organization is about and the current not ideal behaviors that are resulting in additional effort and consumption of resources. Teams must be engaged in discussion around what good looks like and the behaviors behind it.

Leaders, for their part, must be aware of the value of behaviors, their impact on delivering consistent value to customers and they must understand the key systems in the business that support these ideal behaviors. Leaders must also be skilled in their ability to have quality conversation at the right time and in the right way. This last element along with clarity around key business systems are often the missing links and the ones that we explore in the following chapters.

3 Leading the organization

'Just cause you're following a well-marked trail don't mean that whoever made it knew where they were goin''

—Texas Bix Bender, Don't Squat With Yer Spurs On!: A Cowboy's Guide to Life

3.1. Guiding your organization towards deep excellence

From our practical observations and interviews covering many continents and many business sectors the authors can state without question:

The culture of an organization is shaped by the way in which it is led.

Rather than starting at the top to watch leaders and what they do or say, culture is best observed through the activity and behaviors of the front-line teams. These teams can consist of research labs, manufacturing shop floors, or a design house, but the culture behaviors and performance we observe is *always* a direct reflection of the quality and intent of the senior leadership team.

Organizations can get lost in eloquent dissertations about their organizational values and culture but, as mentioned in the previous chapter, they fail miserably to link these desired values and behaviors to the detailed activities that are critical for the organization's success. Many efforts at 'cultural transformation' are undermined further, as leaders and middle managers are disconnected or unsure of their role in living the values, beliefs and behaviors of the organization. There is no link between the values and the way their individual performance is really measured, excluding maybe some self-reflection on whether they have 'lived the values' in an annual or six-monthly appraisal. Equally there is no link or understanding as to why these values and behaviors really influence results!

3.2. *Some fundamental truths of organizational leadership*

To begin the journey to deep excellence leadership must grasp three fundamental truths.

> It is the senior leaders who give direction and influence by their acts or omissions to organizational culture and behaviors.
>
> The direction provided by the senior leadership team is powered (for good or bad) by a middle tier management and supervisory group.

Unfortunately, few organizations grasp the third fundamental truth.

> The real impact of a desired culture and resulting behaviors is only valuable when it manifests itself consistently within the frontline teams. This is where business performance is won or lost.

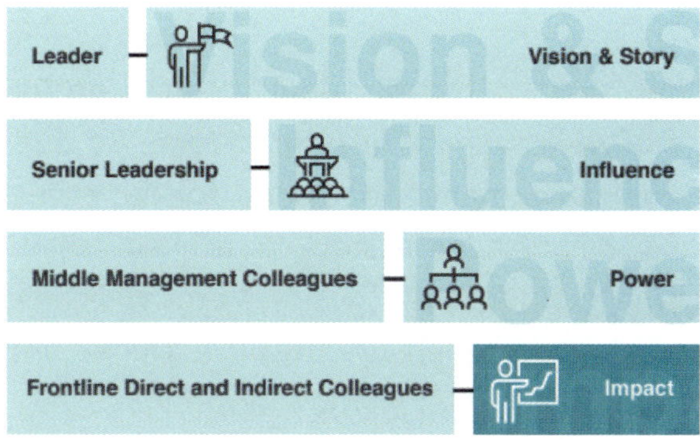

Figure 12: Conversations around vision, culture and behaviors have no value unless we see the impact within value-adding team members of our business. © S A Partners.

To be effective in supporting and enabling any move towards a cultural change. Leaders must clearly define systems that will support their ability to check and validate:

Do individuals understand the purpose of the focus on culture?

Do I see the understanding and drive to achieve this change within the middle management and supervisory groups?

Do we see and hear evidence of the necessary behaviors that are required in the workplace, or in conversations with customers?

Do we see a resulting impact in organizational performance?

Any planned effort to shift the cultural landscape must be supported purposefully by designed systems in the business that will support and continually monitor that sought-after cultural transformation.

This is much more than "change management". Change management to me always seems to have a project mindset approach. This is what we must do. This is how we communicate. This is how we manage risk. This is the timeline...etc.

Thinking in systems allows organizations to focus on the long term and overall purpose of the organizations endeavors. To define systems that will provide ongoing alignment and support for the necessary culture and behavioral transformation necessary to achieve sustainable progress towards that vision and purpose. These systems will come under constant scrutiny and improvement to ensure they are aligned and supporting the expression of the sought-after culture and expressed behavior in the **teams who use them**.

The expression of desired cultural and behavioral transformation is only valuable if the sought-after change in expressed behavior can be observed with the frontline value-adding team members.

3.3. *Finding your story as an organization – the purpose.*

A good example of storytelling and engagement can be heard in the story told of the development of Chobani Yogurt by Hamdi Ulukaya in his 'Anti CEO Play Book' TED Talk in 2019. I have listened to his TED talk many times and watched how the commitment he speaks about has translated directly into actions and the success story of the Chobani business. Hamdi describes meeting the employees of a yogurt factory that was being closed in a rural area of upstate New York. A factory he was about to buy with no money and a seed of an idea (Ulukaya, 2019).

> What hit me the hardest at that time was that this wasn't just an old factory. This was a time machine. This is where people built lives, they left for wars, they bragged about home runs and report cards. But now, it was closing. And the company wasn't just giving up on yogurt, it was giving up on them. As if they were not good enough. And I was shocked how these people were behaving. There was no anger, there were no tears. Just silence. With grace, they were closing this factory. I was so angry that the CEO was far away, in a tower or somewhere, looking at the spreadsheets and closing the factory. Spreadsheets are lazy. They don't tell you about people, they don't tell you about communities. But unfortunately, this is how too many business decisions are made today.
>
> By August 2005, I had the keys for this factory. The first thing I did was to hire four of the original 55 people. I had Maria, the office manager. I had Frank, the wastewater guy. I had Mike, the maintenance guy and Rich, who showed me the plant, the production guy and we had our first board meeting. Mike says, "Hamdi, what are we going to do now?" They look at me as if I have the magic answer. So, I said, "Mike, we're going to go to Ace Hardware store, and we're going to get some paints. And we're going to paint the walls outside." Mike wasn't impressed. He looked at me. He said, "Hamdi, that's fine, we'll do that, but tell me you have more ideas than that."

> I said, "I do. We'll paint the walls white."
>
> In painting those walls, we got to know each other. We believed in each other, and we figured it out together. Five years, me and all my colleagues, we never left the factory. We worked day and night, through the holidays, to fix that plant. The best part of Chobani for me is this: the same exact people who were given up on were the ones who built it back one hundred times better than before. And they all have a financial stake in the company today (Ulukaya, 2019).

Engagement is a contact sport that is directly linked to the work people do and how they do it – and improving the work realizes the genuine story and beliefs of the business.

I also have listened to many other leaders attempt to deliver compelling stories, but unfortunately many fail in their delivery. There is no subsequent rousing of the troops. Individuals' discretionary effort remains locked up. The only nodding heads are those of the executive team. In some cases, there may be an initial flurry of excitement, but this quickly fizzles away, and the status quo reasserts itself like a smug overfed cat reclaiming its favourite resting place!

I feel for these leaders. They often believe in what they are trying to say but they have not truly internalised the vision of the future. In addition, the systems in the business are not robust enough to communicate and support the necessary activity to actively implement the leader's vision in all areas of the business. We will address this in the following chapters as we consider the architecture to support the necessary culture and behaviors that bring real sustainable results.

Story telling is a part of our ancient human culture. Believing the story behind your vision for the organization is a critical point in your journey to deep excellence. Our brains are hardwired to look for leadership. In our stone age past the search for food, safety, shelter for our group must have been a constant preoccupation. We needed leaders to make the final call on where we would go and what we would do. Sometimes these decisions worked, other times they didn't. The trust in our leaders was built on the lived experience resulting from their guidance. Again, our brains are wired to detect any doubt or vagueness in directions we are asked to take.

Figure 13. We are 'wired' to sense doubt in our leader's visions and stories!

If, as a leader, you are going the share a vision of what you believe your organization can be, you have to believe in it <u>and be seen to live it yourself</u>. If you don't, your teams' stone age brain sensors are wired to find you out! The story must also be directly relatable to the teams' lived experience with the colleagues they work with and the community they live in.

> Good – and true- stories told by a company's leaders can shape the culture and brand of a company. A leader's credibility can be severely damaged if they get carried away by storytelling, so that their stories about the market, the company's future prospects and the way it behaves are not consistent with its values and the lived experiences of staff and stakeholders. However, good stories told around the reality of how the organization behaves towards others, how it benefits society as well as customers and shareholders, how it believes in and supports its people, can influence emotions, and help develop strong motivation, commitment and loyalty. (Swart, Chisholm, & Brown, 2015).

There is often a conflict within leaders. They may be responsible for an individual division, site or a team within a larger organization. Often there is a perceived misalignment between the dominant (maybe not ideal) culture in the wider organization and that of the individual leader. The issues may relate to levels of trust and uncertainty around the future structures of the organization. There may be evidence of poor behaviors such as overt or covert conflict or passive aggression. All are visible, observable behaviors that can drive negative consequences within the leader's organization, if the leader allows these behaviors to take the power within the team. It is up to you as the leader to decide how you lead, develop respect, learning and improvement within your site.

It is possible to take the vague statements of values and principles at a corporate level and translate them into something that means something for you and your team. Whatever chaos is happening outside you can define the culture and vision for your team. You define why this local culture is important and how that culture aligns to your aspirations for this team and what you hope to achieve.

Regardless of what part of an organization you work in as a leader, you can frame the culture of excellence within your team. But you must believe your own story.

3.4. Developing your story and aligning it to strategy

When it comes to business strategy, behaviors and leadership it is an unfortunate reality that many businesses fail to connect these three essential elements for success. Three elements that truly support the focused development of a sustainable culture of excellence or Deep Excellence.

Very often they are treated as separate activities owned by different functions in the business.

Strategy: Is often owned by business development or senior corporate teams or sales teams. Or worse again the "Strategy Group".

Behaviors: HR functions or possibly operation excellence. Sometimes in regulated environments this space can be claimed by quality functions who seek a 'Culture of Compliance', 'Right First Time' or the 'Culture of Excellence'.

Leadership: Often left to individual leaders or absorbed into Leadership Development Programmes managed by Learning and Development functions linked to human resources.

While the connection between these three elements is often missing or weak it is not too difficult to begin to align the various mechanisms and systems behind them so that they do connect. We will focus more on the systems piece in the following chapters. For the moment let us consider strategy and behaviors.

3.5. Starting from the top

We see many businesses work hard on strategy. But, unfortunately, it is often the place where objectives of engaging and aligning the organization and the team begin to unravel. They sit down in board rooms and ask, 'OK, so what's our strategy for this year?' While there are some companies who can 'do' strategy well, often what we see is a list of projects with links to cost, quality and delivery which is in effect the day-to-day nuts and bolts running of your business!

To think differently about Strategy, we need to think in terms of storytelling and how words like "Mission" and "Vision" fit into our Story.

We are often faced with leadership teams who are frustrated at lack of ownership or accountability within the organization at all levels. Unfortunately, the only thing we can force people to take ownership and accountability for is their children and their debts! Everything else people must want to own or want to be accountable for.

To achieve this, individuals must invest in and own their part of the story. They must want to play a role and be seen to play that role in their organization – their 'tribe'. Yes, we are back to our tribal communities once again. We want to be part of a tribe and we want to play a part in the tribe's success as that will ensure my own success and survival.

So, how do we think about these three words: Mission, Vision and Strategy, and align our organization to a common story and purpose for our organization?

3.6. Your Mission as an organization:

This is basically the heart and soul of what you do. Sometimes we can get lost in the physical or technical aspects of what we do but this is not your mission.

Figure 13: What would be a compelling Mission statement for a children's orchestra?

Think of a children's orchestra. Is the mission of the orchestra to...?

> Make consistently perfect music performances delivered on time and achieving above 95% satisfaction from audience feedback?

or

> Through the power of music, help develop confidence, skills and friendships that last a lifetime.

Which is more powerful? Which speaks more to the core essence and purpose of a youth orchestra?

Think of a medical device company:

> Working at the forefront of medical technology we develop high quality products that excite our customers and enable them to benefit from best-in-class technologies.
>
> or
>
> We make our surgeons work easier to do so they can improve the health and quality of more people's lives.

Other examples:

Autoliv's Inc who make airbags, seatbelts and steering wheels for cars:

'Providing World Class Life-saving Solutions for Mobility and Society'.

This Mission statement does not mention cars. Its focus is saving lives.

A Dairy Company:

'Create sustainable value for our community of farmer shareholders'.

This dairy company processes cows' milk today, but it could well be other forms of farm produce from vegetable-based milks in the future, to ensure sustainable value to their community of farmer shareholders.

Your Mission should speak to the heart and soul of what you do. Your essence as an organization.

3.7. Your vision of the future:

It is interesting that many companies often speak to Vision first Mission second. Personally, I feel this is a mistake. If the Mission is what we do, our Vision should force us to think about what that Mission will look like in three to five years' time. We call this the 'future vision walk' but it is an exercise that must be purposeful and real.

> *If this is at the heart of what we do, our Mission, what will delivering on that Mission look like in xx years' time?*

Can you draw me the picture of what it will look like? Or better still, walk me through the video of the future business. What products, what technologies, what geographies, what customers would I see? Walk me through the production areas. What will people be doing? What meetings will be taking place and what will be their purpose and who will be at them?

These seem to be very detailed questions to think about, but they are critical to making the vision tangible and real. They also create the foundation for a truly credible story in the business.

We recommend starting this activity by splitting leadership teams into separate groups to draw their own picture and describe their own video. Not surprisingly there can be significant differences! However, we can also find teams who are unanimous on the vision they see. Where there is variation, this is the time to enable open and rich conversation around the differences. There may be differences in priorities. There may be poor alignment between functions with poor communication around key activities and projects.

Where there are differences, it is time to slow the discussion down, ensure a safe space and get all the discussion and potential underlying issues on the table. Getting an aligned vision and story right at this stage saves a lot of frustration, cynicism and wasted effort later.

It is your job as leaders to align with one voice and one story for your team. Any misalignment or doubt will soon be detected by the tribe.

3.8. Visioning example

One of the greatest work experiences I have had occurred while supporting a pharmaceutical company on the west coast of Ireland. The organization had been in existence for over thirty years and was the main employer in the area. During its start-up it was seen as a benchmark state of the art facility. But time, technology and markets moved on and the site was now producing products with limited scope for market development. The leadership team asked us to propose a programme to reinvigorate the site's continuous improvement activity and improve overall site performance.

As with most interventions the activity began with a series of workshops to gain buy in and ownership of the programme with the leadership team. However, it became clear very quickly that there was a back story. There were ongoing discussions at corporate level to divest the site. Technology and markets had shifted, and the value-adding activity provided by the site was no longer there.

The leadership team was working with the corporation to source alternative products for manufacture and seeking investment for process and equipment upgrade. This activity was not really progressing.

The second strategy was to look for a "white horse". An organization that would potentially take over the facility which would basically run as is but with a different name on the gate. The leadership worked with the corporation and local government support agencies to find this white horse; while there were a small number of potential buyers, no white horse seemed to be appearing on the horizon.

This open discussion around the future of the site at times became quite heated. Some of the leadership team felt that not enough was being done to find the white horse. The site leader who was closest to discussions with corporate was more realistic in his outlook. There could be a white horse, but the most likely scenario was that the site would close in three to four years' time.

You could have heard the proverbial pin drop in the room as this news sank in. So here we are, with a leadership team who had been to a large extent responsible for running a site for almost thirty years in a small community on the west coast of Ireland who were now faced with the reality of being responsible for closing the site. In addition, for the next three years the team must remain engaged and focused. There can be no slips in quality, no missed shipments, no safety incidents, or non-compliances. All the usual plates had to keep spinning.

We took a break and resumed the workshop after lunch. On their return the dynamic and energy was very different and not in a good place. I explained that the purpose of today was to develop our vision for the site. While a 'white horse' may yet appear, it is more likely this site will close. I asked the team to draw me a future vision picture of the day the gates of the site will be closed for the final time. Given that this team has been responsible for the best shut down ever! In fact, I referenced the 'Carlsberg' advertising campaign that was running at the time.

> *If Carlsberg did shutdowns, what will make this the best shut down in the world? Probably.*

The team were initially sceptical, but we had won enough trust with them for the team to break into two groups and begin to draw their picture in two separate breakout room. Initially the conversations were muted. But after a short period, the noise level increased. Then there was laughing and joking! What was going on!

The teams reassembled and there was an almost giddy sense of excitement in the room. Amazingly the images that the groups drew were similar but there was one very common image. It showed a party! A celebration: balloons, tents, music, happy people – both employees and the community! Even corporate representatives were there. What caused the turnaround in the team?

We began to break out what was behind each of the images. The answers to my questions were profound and inspiring.

Why are there so many happy people on the day the site is closing for the final time?

Answer: Because no one is afraid for their future. Everyone will have used the time left to build the future they want whether that is a new position in another company, setting up their own business venture or returning to college for further education. No one will be afraid for their future as we have helped to make these new futures possible.

Why are the community people so happy?

Answer: The facility has been providing jobs in the area for over thirty years. The legacy left behind will not be just cleaned up facility and new parkland. We will have worked with the community to create a hub for employment. Our laboratory equipment is top notch, for example. We could help establish a laboratory based analytical centre to sustain and develop jobs in the area. Some of our warehouse space could be donated to the community to facilitate start-up businesses.

What's with the corporate suits?

Answer: They are with us on the day sharing the celebration. The site has performed exceptionally well and beat all previous output and quality targets even though the site is closing down. The team never missed a shipment. The corporate team are also here to facilitate the legacy left to the community. Instead of a PR disaster it is seen as a real win for the corporation and their responsibility to the communities in which they work.

There followed a series of refining workshops to really hone the vision and the associated story. The big test was yet to come. The leadership team had to present and engage the next level down – largely their direct reports, in their vision.

As expected, the white horse was trotted out again. But the leadership team vision was so compelling and spoken to with such passion that this group was soon on the same page. We must do what we need to do as regards our commitment to our customers. But in doing this we ensure that we give the space time and skills to our colleagues so that when the final day comes, no one is concerned about their future.

With the support of the middle management team behind them the team planned a key all-employee meeting. All three hundred and fifty of them. On the day, each member of the leadership team presented a part of the vision. Once each piece was presented the employees were asked to review what they had heard, raise any concerns they may have but also define how they contribute to the story.

It was an incredibly powerful event. More or less, the vision pictures the leadership team drew in that initial workshop session were achieved. Teams became focused on improving efficiency so that time would be available for skill development and career counselling. Team members used the improvement programme to gain accreditation for themselves. Improvement activities also allowed employees to build up their own genuine stories about their continuous improvement activity. Allowing them to speak to their projects with conviction during subsequent job interviews. Robust management systems were put in place to constantly align the team, measure progress, and focus resources in the most critical areas. A wellbeing and coaching programme was developed so that leaders and managers could regularly and effectively check in on people to ensure the 'so, how are you doing?' questions had real meaning and purpose. Closing a site can be an enormously stressful time; leaders and managers had to develop their own personal skills around resilience and coaching skills.

The accumulation of the improvement activity resulted in the site performing at exceptionally high levels. Despite the fact that it was closing they won prizes for its operational excellence activities and employee engagement. Many employees moved on to more senior roles in blue chip multinational organizations. It was indeed a great story and yes there was a party!

Having a picture of the future you desire is one thing, but all visions are exactly that: visions. They will never become reality unless we carefully plan a way to make the vision real by creating a strategy that will engage our team in activities that will make the vision a reality.

3.9. Strategy – the fun starts here!

> A strategy is a way through a difficulty, an approach to overcoming an obstacle, a response to a challenge. If the challenge is not defined it is difficult or impossible to assess the quality of the strategy. If you cannot assess that, you cannot reject a bad strategy or improve a good one.
>
> Despite the roar of voices equating strategy with ambition, leadership, or planning, strategy is none of these. Rather it is a coherent action backed by an argument. The core of a strategist's work is always the same: discover the crucial factors in a situation and design a way to coordinate and focus actions to deal with them.
>
> (Rumelt, 2017).

When we work with leadership teams on their strategy and its execution it always comes back to what was in those future vision pictures. The more detail in the picture the better. Once the future vision is completed and accepted the fun starts! Now we need to figure out how to get there and bring the team with us!

3.10. Skunk Strategies – mischief making at its best!

In our practice, this future visioning is often a pivot point for a leadership team. Often it is the first time they have agreed their personal aspirations for the business in which they work and the team they support. But the real fun starts when the "Skunk Strategies" are uncovered.

Often in multinational organizations competition is encouraged between sites. Standard systems and 'culture' are deployed, score cards, benchmarking and organizational maturity levels are created and compared. Our experience tells us that these approaches seldom sustain. For the simple reason that they in effect supress one of the most valuable behaviors of any group of individuals, the ability to identify a future they aspire to as a group and to make it their own. Telling people the future they will have, is as empty as telling a team to behave a certain way!

If, instead, we ask teams what future they would like for their site and their community, and how this in turn can contribute to the wider corporation, we get a very different picture. I coined the term *Skunk Strategy* from the notion of Skunk Works within Lockheed Martin's research and development activity. Here teams were given time and space to visualise and invent new engines and flying machines of the future many of which are a reality today.

Skunk Strategy allows the local team to paint a picture of their future and make it as real and tangible as possible. It is their picture of what the future could look like. Often the act of drawing out the future picture – even if that future is uncertain –brings new insights and focus to leadership teams. Drawing pictures of what it could look like can often bring certainty and alignment within the leadership team. As stated over again in a forest of management publications, leadership alignment is the starting point for alignment within the wider organization.

It is an incredible moment to watch a leader take the baton and bring their colleagues into a passionately held story. It is transformative. The team begin to form their future vision, their responsibility to their staff and the local community, their responsibility to develop their skills as leaders of this incredible bunch of people in front of them. They make the decision on the future they want to see in their plant, their division, their department. They grasp that future and make it their own. It has become more than work. Now they can tell convincing stories.

In one organization the reality of international cost competitiveness meant their underlying Skunk Strategy was to significantly raise the level of their site's performance, reliability, cost-competitiveness, and adoption of new manufacturing technologies, so their site becomes the preferred site for investment.

This sounds like what every manufacturing site should do! However, in reality, this site had to provide consistent reliable product at a price point below their sister site which was based in a low labour cost economy and was closer to North American Markets.

The Skunk Strategy meant that this European site had to produce significantly greater amounts of product within the existing footprint and create space for new products again without requesting capital investment for new buildings or warehouse space.

The Skunk Strategy meant that any equipment refurbishment or the adoption of new manufacturing technology now had three key targets:

> Increase productivity between sixty-five and eighty-five percent.
>
> Reduce total rolled up manufacturing and logistics cost by thirty percent.
>
> Reduce the footprint used by the equipment by fifty percent.

Consistent quality performance was a given.

This resulted in a move away from long chain driven semi-automated assembly lines, with external inspection points, to fully automated rotating table assembly using robotic pick and place, along with internal inspection by sophisticated vision camera technology.

The freeing up of floor space fed into another key element of the Skunk Strategy for the site. Previously the site did not have close relationships with product managers and product designers. This needed to change. Leaders and managers actively sought out opportunities to meet with and engage with these groups. Attending internal and external product development conferences. Offering support to investigate and resolve product problems. Offering the facility to the organization sales teams and product manager meetings and conferences in the vicinity of the plant. Here, along with the golf, and conference, the visit would include a facilitated tour of the manufacturing site.

These site tours were critical. If there was a product issue a team would be available to walk the product owners through the process. Showing the progress in the investigation and offering <u>already tested</u> solutions to resolve the issue. All employees were made aware that these visits were taking place. Product managers would meet with the employees who made their products. Product managers would attend presentations by the manufacturing teams on the improvements they had made to manufacturing process. Product managers would be blown away by the engagement of the team and the quality of their workspace, and the employees' knowledge of the product and its use. Product managers would also be directed to the empty spaces just waiting to be filled by new products. Sure, where else would they send their new products to?

Hoping for new products to arrive is very different to being confident that they will arrive. Having an ace team ready to seamlessly and confidently deliver either product transfer from another site or a new product and technology was a critical success factor for this strategy. Individuals and teams on this site had been involved in product transfers before. Some of them had gone well others not so. The leadership pulled together various team members of these previous product transfer and new product introduction projects. They brainstormed the issues that made them work well and the problems.

Some of problems are listed below:

- Site team not involved early enough in planning and design of the product or transfer plan

- Insufficient due diligence on technology services and licensing and regulatory requirements and changes to packaging design and content
- Transfer driven by transferring site not the receiving site
- Bad vibes and little technical support from the transferring site
- Unrealistic planning timelines
- Not enough thought put into pre-transfer inventory builds

The list went on. But with this list in hand, the team put in place the best product transfer team in the corporation. This team were confident in their abilities and experience and were able to prevent potential issues by identifying them at the early planning stages. They became known for their excellent work.

One of the interesting developments by the team was countering the negative vibes from the existing transfer site. This was addressed through a very human approach. The team took the stance of understanding the very real sense of failure and loss felt by the transferring site and team. The team understood it because they had been the "victims" of transfers in the past. To counter this, the team developed very personal relationships with the site very early on, visiting the site in small groups way in advance of the transfer. The transfer team consisted of operators from the receiving department who travelled to the transfer site. They worked shoulder to shoulder with the local team, being helpful, supporting them by going beyond the work at hand, and helping where they could with other activity on the transferring site.

The transfer team also shared knowledge with the local site about manufacturing practices and systems from their home site. In doing so, they gave the local site and individuals skills and knowledge that could be applied within the transferring site or wherever they ended up as individuals. Relationships were built, parties were had, and team photographs were taken.

The leadership team of the receiving site were clear in their Skunk Strategy. If they wanted to be *the* site to take in new products or existing product portfolios from other sites, they needed to have the teams and systems in place to do so flawlessly. They needed to understand and manage all associated stakeholders in the product and process to be transferred or introduced.

The example above is from almost twenty years ago. But the site is still in existence while the site in the low-cost location closed a long time ago. The European site has grown in employee numbers threefold. To this day, it is still receiving inward capital investment and new product portfolios from the corporation.

Whatever the situation in your business to create real and lasting cultural change, the leadership community must be able to speak convincingly to their agreed vision for where they want to bring the site and the teams who work within it. But having a vision is not enough. You need to make your vision a reality through focused activity as we have seen above. This activity must engage every member of your organization in achieving the critical success factors that will make the story real.

That is when a strategy becomes truly real in every part of the organization.

3.11. *Critical Success Factors. Making that future vision a reality.*

To help clarify what is needed to deliver on a vision we use the term Critical Success Factors (CSFs), sometimes known as "Must Win Battles". These are the few vital areas at which we must excel to secure the future vision.

These CFSs must encompass every part of the business and provide focus on the "vital few" things that will realize our vision. Typically, there will be between five and eight in number.

Descriptions of the CSFs are aspirational but are intended to provide the focus for daily actions across the organizations.

CSFs can be predicated by 'the ability to...'

> 'The ability to build close long term client relationships delivering exceptional value'
>
> 'The ability to rapidly respond to new service or product opportunities'

Or they can be a simple doing statement...

> 'Working mutually with our customers'
>
> 'Engage every member of the business in making tomorrow better than today'
>
> "Develop teams' skills in relation to automation of operational and support process"

Whatever the CSFs are, they should address the things that may be missing, underperforming, or introducing risk into the organization's ability to achieve the future vision applicable to the whole organization.

As a process to identify CSFs with a leadership team we use a simple cascade model. With the vision picture on the wall and visible to the leadership team, we ask each member to take some silent time and write down what they believe are the top three CSFs, and to define the ones they believe are most important.

Everyone is then asked to choose a partner and, working in pairs, agree a joint proposal for **FOUR** ideas by combination or elimination of the factors each has presented.

The pairs then merge into groups of six and work in these groups to agree a joint proposal for **FIVE** ideas by combination or elimination.

All the resulting proposals are presented together and the whole team work to produce a final list of **SEVEN** or **EIGHT** ideas.

This is a very powerful activity to ensure alignment within the leadership group. It is important that a consensus is gained on these CSFs as they will be used to define priorities across the whole organization. They will also form part of the senior leadership team's high level score card. A three-year vision is made up of thirty-six months of activity and the constant review of that activity.

Once the initial set of CSFs are available, they should be subject to the following tests.

Are they:

- Necessary and sufficient to achieve the vision
- Clearly signaling the strategic direction towards the vision
- Clear, concise, and singular in their focus they should be applicable to all levels and written in a form that is meaningful to all
- Potentially motivational for the team
- Potentially measurable in a format to visualize progress or are linked to KPIs that signal the impact of team's focus

The link to measures that matter is critical. The critical success factors once defined must then go through a process of Key Performance Indicator (KPI) cascade. For each CSF there will be lagging indicators, the high level KPIs, that tell us if we have or have not hit expectations. But, more importantly, the leading indicators must be defined – as these will form part of the cascade into one of the most important systems within any business: the tiered management structure. We will review this critical system in detail in chapter seven.

3.12. Pulling it together:

Leaders own and are responsible for the prevalent level of performance and culture in the organization. Efforts to change prevailing culture must begin at senior level. There must be clarity on the purpose and future vision of the business and senior leadership must be absolutely committed to that vision and the story that supports it.

The story must be shared. Team members must be given the opportunity to contribute and define the part of the story they can play in order to make the story real. It is only then can we begin to discuss the behaviors at each level that are necessary to impact day-to-day performance in a positive way.

The agreed future vision must be broken down into the Critical Success Factors necessary to make that vision a reality. These CSFs must be cascaded through the business in the form of leading measures and behavioral indicators with gives ownership of the CSFs to frontline teams. The system that supports this process is the tiered management and the leadership systems that constantly review alignment and engagement at all levels of the business.

4 Deep Excellence self and leadership

4.1. Your personal role as a leader

'The world will see you as you see you and treat you the way you treat yourself'

-Beyoncé

There are many books and reference materials out there listing the qualities of an impactful leader. Broadly speaking they can be broken into two categories the things leaders do and the way they are. If we list just some of the collection of words that are often attributed to impactful leadership, we come up with the following:

The things leaders do, create purpose, share vision, set goals, hold people to account, make good decisions, empower, and motivate others, manage complexity, build and promote teams, learn and share, lead by example, communicate effectively build trust, drive out fear. We have covered many of these in earlier chapters.

The way leaders are, transparent, gritty, accountable, high integrity, self-managing, adaptable, empathetic, self-aware, courageous, curious, passionate, creative, humble, resilient.

In their book, *Neuroscience for Leadership*, Swart, Chisholm and Brown describe what our brains need from leadership.

> Our brain needs a leader to create environments that feel safe and certain, even when the world is far from either. We also need leaders who communicate well, who make understanding them easy, who create processes that are fair and transparent, so our brains do not waste precious effort second guessing them or trying to understand what to do next.
>
> We want leaders to help us give meaning to our lives, who demonstrate that they value us (...) good relationships are

> absolutely critical to our wellbeing, so our brains need leaders who develop supportive relationships in which we can innovate, create and develop ourselves.
>
> (Swart, Chisholm, & Brown, 2015)

This is a tall order for any individual but not impossible. Some of us fall into leadership positions while some of us seek it out. Either way it can be an amazingly rewarding and fulfilling position to be in. But equally its associated responsibility and pressures can break people. Therefore, leaders must also learn to be adaptable.

Leaders today engage in a multitude of diverse and complex activities. These could span from accepting new roles and responsibilities, to taking organizations to new heights, to navigating tremendous internal and external pressures to adopt new ways of thinking around diversity, equity, and inclusion, or directing the efforts of an organization to divest parts of itself to make space for a new venture. In each of these circumstances, leaders might find themselves in situations where the problem's solution is not easily obtained and is often elusive. Solving them will require the leader's dedication, perseverance, and grit, along with a sense of personal purpose, to motivate themselves and others to engage in the work ahead.

Ronald Heifetz, Alexander Grashow, and Marty Linksy emphasized the importance of adaptability in leadership (Heifetz, Grashow, & Linksy, 2009)

The challenges the world faces today are not , they suggest,

> amenable to authoritative expertise, although people might hope that if the right subject matter expert could only be found, these problems would be solved. These are what we call adaptive challenges, gaps generated by bold aspirations amid challenging realities. For these, the world needs to build new ways of being and responding beyond the current repertories of available know-how. What is needed from a leadership perspective are new forms of improvisational expertise, a kind of process expertise that knows prudently how to experiment with never-been-tried-

> before relationships, means of communication, and ways of interacting that will help people develop solutions that build upon and surpass the wisdom of today's experts.
>
> The answers cannot come only from on high. The world needs distributed leadership because the solutions to our collective challenges must come from many places, with people developing micro-adaptations to all the different micro-environments of families, neighbourhoods, and organizations around the globe
>
> (Heifetz, Grashow, & Linksy, 2009, pp. 2-3)

Leaders that understand and adapt their leadership to the changing demands and dive deeper into the organization for solutions, fare much better than leaders that focus solely on directing the work. As you embrace the idea of adaptability, you become more influential as you exercise leadership throughout the organization.

Our experience within our global consulting practice suggests to us that good leaders thrive on six energies.

- The deep conviction and belief in what they are trying to achieve. Their story.
- A constant desire to learn.
- Willingness to adapt
- Empathy for their teams.
- Respect for their own personal health space.
- Resilience.

4.2. Finding your personal story

As the overall site leader or the leader of a function you must internalise this story and vison for yourself. As a functional leader you must be able to relate the story and vision into something that is relevant to your team.

If you can't there is something wrong with the story and you need to review this with those who presented it.

In an ideal world functional leaders play a central role in developing and validating the story and vision. But in the heat of the moment and the often-exciting debates that arise in the formation of the story you may not have had time to internalise it yourself.

That is all perfectly fine. But if after internalising it, and something still doesn't fit, speak up. You have to be able to deliver that story with conviction to your team and work with them to identify how they contribute to the defined critical success factors and measure their impact on them. If the story and vision doesn't fit with you, it certainly won't work for your team. Have the necessary conversation to ensure you can align with the story. It must become your story and that of your team.

However, taking the organizational story and tying it to your story is only possible if you have taken steps to understand what you believe in and what's important to you.

Bill George (2015) is the renowned author of *Discover Your True North*. In it, he details his interviews with several prominent leaders and how they used their personal life stories to deepen their leadership commitment and resilience (George, 2015).

In each interview, George found that leaders who were truly inspiring understood their life stories by embracing both the positive and negative aspects to learn about what was important to them. They then matched their aspirations with the company's to create tremendous momentum in their respective marketplaces.

In our experience, we have seen individuals come to understand their personal stories by:

1. Looking at patterns from their earlier life to determine which events, people, and experiences had the most significant impact

2. Determining in which experiences they found the most incredible inspiration

3. Reframing failures or disappointments as learning and growth experiences and

4. Resolving to make adjustments to their behaviors as a result of their reflections

You can then integrate the organization's story when you find and understand your personal story and what's important to you. Then, with your story fully present, you can carry the organization's vision with passion and purpose, thus energizing those around you.

4.3. The desire to learn and adapt

'You aren't learning anything when you are talking'

-Lyndon B. Johnson

I am often astonished how little time leaders spend developing themselves. I don't know who is reading all these leadership books? College students? Writers of Leadership books? But it is seldom leaders in my experience. They may do some courses because HR told them to! Seldom do we see the practical application of materials covered in these courses.

Organizations often forget that the very places where we need to apply good leadership skills is also the place where we can learn and practice these skills.

The ratio 70-20-10 is often used as a model for learning and within organizations. Individuals obtain 70 percent of their knowledge from practical work-related experiences, 20 percent from interactions with colleagues, and 10 percent from formal classroom learning environments. This learning model was framed in the 1980s by three researchers: Morgan McCall, Michael M. Lombardo and Robert A. Eichinger, who were researching the developmental experiences of successful managers. The research was captured in Lombardo and Eichinger's book, *The career architect development planner* (Lombardo & Eichinger, 1996).

In their research following multiple interviews with managers and leaders, McCall, Lombardo and Eichinger suggest that hands-on experience (the seventy percent) is the most beneficial for learners as it enables them to hone their job skills through the decisions they make and the observed consequences. They learn how to exert influence effectively within their teams but also how they interact with and influence their leaders. Most importantly they learn through their mistakes through trial and error and the immediate feedback that takes place at the coal face.

The influence of others on the learner is captured in the twenty percent element. This interaction takes place through a range of activities that include social mores, formal mentoring and coaching activity, shared learning through activities such as a problem-solving or planning activity. Communication and feedback to the learner is an important part of this learning environment and needs to be formalised.

Only ten percent of effective skill and knowledge development can be expected to come from formal classroom or online training and educational activity.

Seems obvious but for a leader to learn they must open their mind to learning. A prerequisite for this is humility.

> One common trait among leading practitioners of organizational excellence is a sense of humility. Humility is an enabling principle that precedes learning and improvement. A leader's willingness to seek input, listen carefully, and continuously learn creates an environment where team members feel respected and energized and will give freely of their creative abilities. Improvement is only

> possible when people are willing to acknowledge their vulnerability and abandon bias and prejudice in their pursuit of a better way.
>
> The Shingo Institute principle- Lead with Humility (Shingo, 2022)

Another part of learning is adapting to new information we receive from seeking input and listening. Heifetz et al. (2009) state that the best way to begin the adaptation process is to *get on the balcony* so that you can see what is truly happening in your team or organization.

For example, a leader can initiate the adaptive process by examining how an organization's compensation, promotion, reward, and recognition systems encourage or discourage behaviors. The leader could then deeply reflect on how well those newly formed behaviors support the organization's strategic goals and direction.

With this information, the leader could approach the team with the organization's mission and dialogue with them about how they feel the organization's systems are impacting behavior. The team could then list organizational structures, behaviors, and practices that are supporting or impeding the mission.

After completing both exercises, the leader is ready to engage in the adaptive work of change. They are prepared with not only their take on the situation but now have the information from those close to the processes to understand which direction is best and what could be changed to achieve the desired state.

In this way, the leader looked at the organization from a balcony view and received the necessary information and support to engage effectively in the change work that needs to be done. A leader can quickly lose the confidence of the team if they are seen to lack the complete picture. However, armed with the wider view, leaders can see the various avenues to resolve and provide purposeful support to their team.

All we need to learn about the effective and efficient management of a business is within the business itself. We just need to Go See and Listen to the workplace, that is where we learn. The insights discovered are what make up a true learning organization. However, the leadership learning process must be aligned with key business systems which, as we will discuss, place leadership learning as an integral part of the participative cultural transformation of an organization.

4.4. *Empathy*

Empathy is one of the key foundations of emotional intelligence.

> For a leader.. it doesn't mean adopting other people's emotions as one's own and trying to please everybody. That would be a nightmare and make action impossible. Rather, empathy means thoughtfully considering employee's feelings – along with other factors- in the process of making good decisions.
>
> (Goleman, 1998)

Empathy is not a sensitivity to individuals' feelings and emotions, but the ability to feel as they do and 'take a walk in their shoes'.

But again, there is a warning on the impact of our brain's tendency to conserve energy and take short cuts.

> If I am empathetic and can feel your pain at your loss, I may express myself in ways which show respect, maintain your dignity and make what I say easier for you to hear and deal with. I may think of more options of help the organisation can offer. But my brains tendency to make guesses and take energy saving shortcuts, together with sheer variety and individuality of people mean that I might also be very wrong.
>
> (Swart, Chisholm, & Brown, 2015)

Peter Senge et al. (1994) would describe this way of thinking as part of the *Ladder of Inference* model, from former Harvard Professor, Chris Argyris created (Argyris, Putnam, & McClain, 1985) (Senge, 2006).

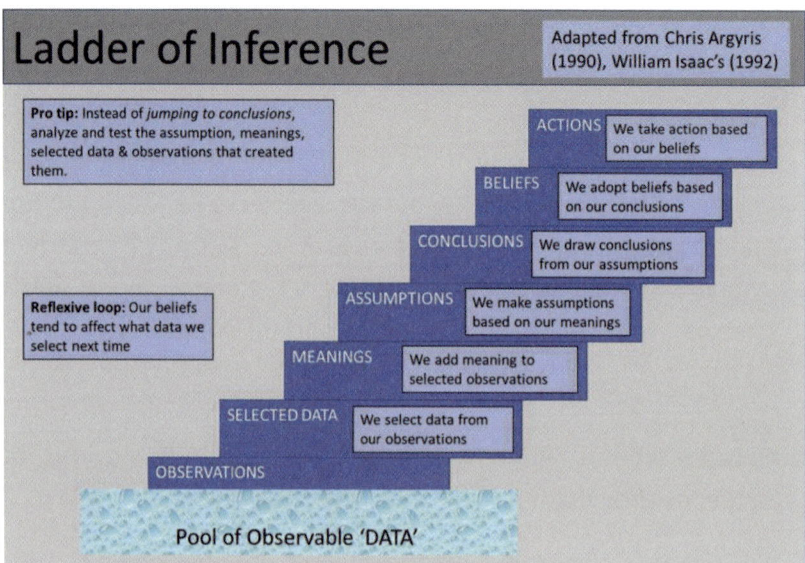

The ladder of inference is built upon the idea that we typically believe that

1. Our beliefs are the truth.
2. The truth is obvious.
3. Our beliefs are based on accurate data.
4. The data we select is the real data.

It typically follows this pattern: 1) we observe behavior, 2) select only elements of the behavior to focus on, 3) add meaning based on the data we selected, 4) make assumptions based on the meanings we assigned, 5) draw conclusions based on our assumptions 6) adopt beliefs based on the conclusions we have made, 7) take action based on those beliefs, and 8) reinforce the way we interpret behaviors based on previous experience to enhance our ability to make conclusions faster.

However, there is a fundamental flaw in this thinking in that our perspective only describes one narrative surrounding a situation.

Therefore, the best way to establish an empathetic mindset is to shift away from our intuitive nature to act based on our beliefs and move toward a more inclusive model that focuses on ensuring a common understanding of the observable data before climbing up the rest of the ladder (Argyris, Putnam, & McClain, 1985).

For example, let's say you have an employee that is late for a meeting you chair and sat down without acknowledging their tardiness or apologizing. Instead of asking questions to understand why the employee was late, you may focus on the fact that the employee was late and did not apologize. In the past, you have experienced that when people are late, they typically care little about the person running the meeting; therefore, you assume that the employee also feels the same way and is purposefully inconsiderate. You then erroneously conclude that the person's professionalism must be corrected and resolve to speak to them about their lack of professionalism and insist that they improve their punctuality.

In just a few moments, you have climbed up the *ladder of inference* and made a decision based on misguided assumptions and beliefs. This process is reinforced by one's *reflexive loop*. The more one comes to their erroneous conclusions, the more their beliefs about how people work become solidified. Once this happens, they may automatically determine that any behavior that resembles their previous experience must mean the same thing in their current situation.

This way of thinking is counterproductive and reduces our ability to feel empathy. The way to stop our quick ascension up the *ladder* is to follow these four steps:

1. Become more aware of our thinking and reasoning (reflection)
2. Make our thinking and reasoning more visible to others by letting them know what is on our minds and how we are interpreting a particular action or conversation (advocacy)

3. Inquiring into others' thinking and reasoning to better refine our data or observations and enhance our understanding of them (inquiry)

By following these three steps, we create an inclusive culture that will allow us to understand the interpersonal or intragroup dynamics, thus avoiding miscommunication and conflict while building empathetic relationships.

Empathy done well allows us to build trust as we communicate to understand and relate our story to individuals and teams, and we are open, and actively listening to their responses. To avoid the risk of making assumptions we need to communicate, and we need to listen. In doing so we strengthen relationships and build rapport and trust with our team. We identify opportunities to close skills gap that may be a cause for concern and discover opportunities for real sustainable improvements that can be led by the team.

4.5. Personal Health and Space

There is ample advice available on good diet and fitness so there is no need to repeat that here. The only point to make here is not to ignore the importance of it for you and your work in leading and influencing your team.

Physical fitness can be an issue for many executives given the time spent in the office, car, or meetings. The link between physical fitness and mental health is well documented. Enough said.

But what about your personal space, family, and personal time. At a certain time in my own career, I was regularly woken during the night due to issues at a plant. It was not frequent enough to be a major problem but on occasion I did need to attend the plant. However, one week it did become an issue as I was called three nights in a row.

As usual, it took someone close to me to point out how ridiculous this situation was. I wasn't even getting paid, and I still turned up for work the next day! But up to that critical week I was comfortable enough with the calls. It showed I had an important role to play. People relied on me, and I was helping them solve problems.

But I wasn't really. I was teaching the team a form of learned helplessness.

The three-call week revealed what a poor manager I had been. There were no real systems in place. Teams were not taking ownership. How could they as there were no real procedures in place to tell them what to do. Most of them were in my head!

Fuelled by the *'this can **NEVER** happen again'* conversation which ensued when I got home at two am after call number three, I set about defining systems and procedures. I trained teams and trained trainers of teams. I established escalation protocols and schedules to cover shift patterns and absences. The new systems took time to bed in and there were some calls, but none required a visit to the plant. After four weeks: no more calls.

As leaders and managers, we can often get pulled into the hero mode as I did. It can feel good, but it is not a healthy place to be. In reality, it means that we are not doing our jobs right. We compensate for our poor work by sacrificing our personal time.

I sometimes use the leaders / manager out of work support time as a key behavioral measure! Why are the teams calling on you to solve problems? Why are you supporting a culture of learned helplessness? What needs to be in place to stop the calls FOREVER!

Your own space is precious as is the time you have alive on this planet. I had a call with a work colleague one evening planning work for the next day. He died that night of a brain haemorrhage. We work to live, not live to work.

Mind your personal time. Fix systems and enable teams to solve their own problems. There is always tomorrow to debrief, learn and improve.

4.6. *Personal resilience.*

ROSENCRANTZ We think not so, my lord.

HAMLET Why, then, 'tis none to you, for there is nothing either good or bad, but thinking makes it so. To me it is a prison.

Hamlet (Act II, Scene ii, 267-9)

Taking on a leadership or management role in any organization is certain to result in personal and team setbacks. Resilience is the ability to bounce back from these setbacks and move on. However, high levels of personal resilience can not only allow us to bounce back but take advantage of the setback (Margolis & Stoltz, 2010).

There are many ways in which you can build your personal resilience to help deal with stress. Diet and fitness certainly help as do friendship circles and support outside of work setting. Getting good quality sleep is an important element. Shut off times and regular habits before bedtime can all help relax the mind before bed. Altruism and counting your blessing can help put setbacks in perspective. In addition, activities that provide a sense of personal achievement and control help to build up your personal buffer bank or resilience.

You can teach yourself to breathe into the stress associated with the setback and recognize that it will pass. Using the mindfulness practice of taking time to 'sit with the difficult' and breathe into the issue can allow you identify strategies to deal with the setback and identify possible opportunities.

In *Neuroscience for Leadership* Swart et al. (2015) describe how being in charge of organizations in times of turbulence can be challenging, stressful and lonely. Managing that stress and not passing it on to team members, while maintaining high standards of performance requires high levels of performance. The authors cite interesting research by Sherman et al. indicating that higher level executives do not necessarily have higher levels of the stress hormone cortisol in their system. They suggest that lower stress levels in leaders may be a factor in the attainment of these high positions or because of it (Sherman, et al., 2012).

Having a structure process for looking for the opportunity in adversity is a useful mechanism to reduce the impact of stressful event on the wider team. The purposeful change of mindset moves individuals from reflexive, cause oriented think to active, response orientated thinking. Margolis and Stoltz proposed a structured approach to mindset change focusing on the four lenses of resilience control, impact, breadth, and duration, . (Margolis & Stoltz, 2010)

Cause – Oriented Thinking	**Response-Oriented Thinking**
Control	
Was this adverse event inevitable, or could I have prevented it?	What features of the event can I (even potentially) improve?
Impact	
Did I cause the adverse event, or did it result from external sources?	What sort of positive impact can I personally have on what happens next?
Breadth	
Is the underlying cause of this event specific to it or more widespread?	How can I contain the negatives of the situation and generate currently unseen positives?
Duration	
Is the underlying cause of this event enduring or temporary?	What can I do to begin addressing the problem now?

Figure 14: Strengthening Resilience through Structured Thinking (Margolis & Stoltz, 2010).

Through a series of questions around each of the elements the authors build their structured resilience regime to move leaders and managers to action orientated thinking where they take control and seek the opportunities arising from the adversity.

> Managers need to shift from this kind of reflexive thinking to "active" thinking about how best to respond, asking themselves what aspects they can control, what impact they can have, and

> how the breadth and duration of the crisis might be contained. Three types of questions can help them make this shift.
>
> Specifying questions help managers identify ways to intervene, the more specific the answers, the better. Visualizing questions help shift their attention away from the adverse event and toward a more positive outcome. Collaborating questions push them to reach out to others—not for affirmation or commiseration but for joint problem solving. Each type of question can clarify each of the four lenses of resilient thinking.
>
> (Margolis & Stoltz, 2010)

In applying this model, leaders exercise a part of a set of strategies collectively known as self-leadership (Cutliff, 2022). Self-leadership is the execution of behaviors that empower individuals to influence themselves to action. Thus, taking control of their situation rather than being controlled by it. The author notes that those who engage in self-leadership practices have been shown to have higher levels of self-efficacy, hope, optimism, resilience, and work engagement.

Those skilled in self-leadership deploy two types of strategies to enhance their ability to influence themselves to action positively:

1. Behavioral
2. Cognitive focused strategies

Behavioral self-leadership strategies focus on increasing leaders' self-awareness of their behavioral propensities to achieve desired outcomes. For example, a leader might observe how their behavior impacts the preferred result. Once patterns are identified, they may then engage in self-goal setting in which they either make a goal for a new behavior or to achieve a more reasonable outcome. Next, to encourage their continued pursuit of the goal, they engage in self-reward setting in which they select something that increases their happiness and ties that reward to the achievement of the goal. Lastly, they would engage in self-cueing behavior in which they set up reminders to encourage them to engage in certain behaviors while minimizing distracting behaviors or actions.

As they do this, they take control of their environment, thus energizing themselves to achieve the ideal outcomes.

Cognitive self-leadership strategies emphasize the focus on improving one's internal state to increase one's confidence and feelings of self-efficacy. For example, a leader may focus on a task's more naturally rewarding aspects. This strategy is typically enacted by searching for which part of the activity ties directly to their purpose or belief system. Another strategy a leader might employ is mental imagery or visualization. When a problematic task presents itself, a leader can significantly improve their ability to achieve it by practicing successful outcomes before engaging in the specific activity or task. This activity will enhance their ability to react positively to a number of challenging stimuli or activities. A third strategy is that a leader may engage in positive self-talk in which they review their internal monologues. In doing this, they become more aware of how their monologues are either irrational, pessimistic, or defeating and replace them with more optimistic or functional ones. Lastly, leaders that fully embrace the cognitive strategies look for ways to shape their beliefs and assumptions positively and strive to eliminate the dysfunctional thinking patterns and lead to mental states that are depressive or otherwise ineffective (e.g., all or nothing thinking, focusing on only negative feedback, or dismissing successes as mere luck).

The most resilient individuals tend to use several of these strategies to propel themselves to high performance. As leaders learn to observe, reflect, interpret, and intervene on their behavior, they become better able to handle setbacks and bounce back from them as they strive to achieve their personal and organizational goals.

Building resilience in the way leaders respond to adverse situations and support their team through these difficult times is an important skill all leaders need to develop. It is during these challenging times your team seek leadership and direction. They are the times when ancient processes that drive fear and uncertainty can dominate the majority of thinking. Resilience allows leaders to learn from previous challenges and build on that learning as they guide their teams through new challenges.

4.7. Pulling it together.

As a leader, like it or not, you cast a shadow into your organization, your tribe. Our stone age brains are still wired to watch and take signals, no matter how subtle, from our leadership.

> Can I trust the leader with my loyalty?
>
> Is this decision a safe option for me and my offspring?
>
> Will this mean more and better food?

Your ability to manage yourself, your behaviors, and how you deal with adversity are all under the scrutiny of your tribe. The skill of understanding and managing yourself is vital for your own and your organization's journey towards deep excellence.

5 Developing and deploying ideal behaviors.

5.1. Behaviors, culture and the bottom line

One of the first questions we need to ask ourselves when we raise the age-old discussion around culture, values and behaviors is, why are behaviors so important? What should drive us to really consider culture and behaviors?

Organizations often gain comfort in the absence of a behavioral focus by looking at business results over the last few years and thinking...

> 'You know what? We're doing okay. We have ups and downs but in general, we hit our targets without all this focus on culture and behaviors.'

We come across this thinking all too often. Maybe we should consider, okay, we are getting results. But how much effort has it taken us? Could we have made it easier to get these results and maybe even better results? Remember the exercise we mentioned in chapter two: our thought experiment with leadership teams to reflect on how much better things could be.

Another version of the values discussion is 'The Corporate Programme'. The 'Corporation' have decided what our values and behaviors need to be. We (the site) have a timeline to communicate these goals and explain them to our teams. As a site, we also have a timeline (usually short) to incorporate these new values into every individual's personal development plan and annual review. These new values and behaviors have been developed by cross-functional focus groups in some part of the world. Where there is a need for local translations, the team have ensured the 'values & behaviors' have the appropriate 'localization' context to aid interpretation.

Hands up, how many people have seen those programmes really work? Or how many people have embarked on such a programme only to find that the 'core values' change when a new leader is in the seat? Sure, they generate plenty of bum bags, pens, tee shirts and a variety of other landfill packers but they have little lasting impact. The local culture and behavior in the workplace generally remains the same. It may even become a little more jaundiced as yet another cultural-change initiative disappears into the wallpaper.

These situations are hugely frustrating for local leadership teams and can result in an erosion of trust in any focus on values and behaviors, often leading to 'Here we go again' dialogues within front line teams.

When we begin to discuss values, beliefs and behaviors within organizations, we often forget that we are, in effect, trying to 'get inside' people's heads and hearts! My head tends to be a very personal and important space for me. I have personal values that either motivate or demotivate me. I am my best self when my environment and social circle align well with my own beliefs and values. If I meet individuals or organizations that clash with my core values and beliefs, I can sometimes get involved in stimulating conversations where I can learn and expand – or modify – my value and belief system. However, where there is fundamental core misalignment, I tend not to spend too much time with these organizations or individuals. I might be able to tolerate the situation for a while but generally not for long!

There is a growing movement toward a very different approach to thinking about behaviors and culture and it must start at a site level. By site I mean the office real or virtual, that we go to. The factory where we work together to make, cars, drugs, ready meals or garments. It is the hospital or educational establishment where we cure and educate people. These individual sites may be part of wider corporate organizations, but it is the actual expressed culture and behaviors within that individual site that count.

Many of the values expressed at corporate level may echo true within the site, however, the day-to-day, week to week performance of the site is dependent on the values and expressed behaviors required at that site.

The actions we can see and the conversations we can hear, within the teams at the individual organization level, are necessary to ensure the consistent and efficient delivery of value to that site's customers.

5.2. Some hard personal learning on what behaviors can look like.

The behaviors and culture we seek must be aligned to the work that we do.

This was brought home to me a long time ago. I was supporting a pharmaceutical manufacturer in Dublin, Ireland. We were dealing with a challenging cultural environment. The teams had been doing what they were doing for a long time. Teams and individuals had become set in their ways but now the organization needed to radically change its levels of performance and contribution to the wider corporate network. Our team in S A Partners were there to help with that change.

There were concerns about the pervading culture on site and we began to facilitate discussions within work groups around process performance and the behaviors that can either help or hinder that performance. The organization was using the Shingo Model of Enterprise Excellence as a guide to support the necessary cultural change. See www.Shingo.org for more information on the model and the philosophy behind its approach.

The Shingo Enterprise Excellence Guiding Principles were used as means to discover what ideal behaviors are necessary to ensure a safe, effective and efficient work environment. I was working in a chemical process area with a process team reviewing the principle *Respect Every Individual*. We discussed the principle by reading the definition and drawing out what Respect Every Individual would look like in this work environment. There were some good discussions but relatively shallow. I asked one senior gentleman, who had been quiet and was obviously just about tolerating the whole situation, for his thoughts.

With a gasp of exasperation and a few colourful expletives he gave his thoughts. It was a while ago, but the conversation has stayed with me!

> 'Respect you say? Don't talk to me about F***n respect! I'll tell you what respect means for me. Ya see that shovel on the wall over there. I can spend thirty minutes looking for that F***n shovel! I need it to transfer material into the vessel. It's spark proof, and I have to use **that** shovel, but it regularly goes missing! It happens all the time here. And it's not just the F***n shovel. Other tools go missing too!
>
> If I cannot find the right tools, I get delayed with the mix and the batch is late! Why can't we have enough tools so that everyone has what they need!'

For this gentleman showing respect was simple. He knew what he needed to do in his work. He was experienced and wanted to do good work. Respect for every individual to him meant that equipment had to be in the right place to allow him to do what he needed to do at the time he needed to do it.

It was a great moment for the team and the site. It allowed the team to really focus on what behaviors were preventing the team from doing what they needed to do.

> *I show respect for my colleague by always returning tools to their designated location and only using tools that are designated for my work area.*

On the surface this situation seemed to be a relatively easy fix. Get the right equipment in the right place. Colour code it so the department can be identified. However, this would **not have been enough**. This issue was a significant source of frustration for the team, and it had been going on for **many years**! The team had mentioned it before, **but nothing happened**.

5.3. *The role of Leaders*

From this simple example we began to unravel wider issues around behaviors on the site. How were leaders and managers interacting with their teams? How often do they go to the shop floor? What do they talk about or do when they get there?

We could have put in systems of visual management with checks in place to ensure tools and equipment were in the right place and available at the right time, but it would have failed within a few months.

We first had to gain awareness and alignment with leaders and managers that the placement and availability of tools was an important 'work system'. This work system played a critical role in the team's ability to perform. Leaders show respect for the work system by being aware that it is there! By having conversations about how it might be improved and listening to and supporting those improvements.

Most importantly, leaders need a high level of sensitivity to notice situations when the system is not working or not being respected - not waiting to be told this is the case but being present in the work area and asking questions.

Visual management as a principle in a workplace should be about enabling the workplace to 'speak to us'. Leaders must be able to understand the language and see evidence of issues for themselves. Leaders must be sensitive to the signals visual management systems can give while they are truly present in the work areas. Not waiting to be told there are problems, but by being proximate to and present in the work. Having the courage and confidence to ask the right questions in the right way is a critically important leadership skill which we cover in chapter seven.

5.4. *Opening the dialogue around behaviors:*

While it is often suggested that we should look at good and not so good behaviors, in most situations it is easier for teams to identify the not so good behaviors. Teams tend to understand the issues that are causing frustration or delay. But once we begin to tackle and discuss these not ideal behaviors, it is amazing how simple it is to move the conversation to what ideal behaviors look like!

An example might be useful from a time and fees business. The back-office team were asked to describe some of the not ideal behaviors impacting on the performance of the business:

> 'I cannot issue invoices because the time sheets for the teams are late and often inaccurate. Often, I must chase people multiple times. They do not seem to relate timesheets to the invoicing process. The longer invoices are outstanding, the higher the debt we carry so cashflow is reduced.'

So, what would be ideal behaviour?

> 'Timesheets are always completed for Monday morning each week and if there is likely to be an issue it is flagged as early as possible.'

In this situation, the business ran some training and awareness sessions on the link between timesheets, invoicing, and debt and the subsequent impact on cashflow. However, this alone would not have been enough. A work system was put in place to create greater visibility on timesheet error and on time completion. The value of showing respect for colleagues was observable through the behaviour of completing timesheets on time. Individual performance was reviewed during 1:1 meetings with managers and became part of individual overall performance assessment.

The behaviors we look for must be aligned to the work that we do. Here, no matter how well the team performed for their clients, if the invoicing process did not work effectively and accurately, the business could fail. Taking the value as Respect, was translated into a very real observable behaviour which if absent, caused real difficulty for the business and the bottom line.

> **If we want to change behavior we have to look at the systems in the business that either enable or disable the behavior we need.**

5.5. Deploying behaviors in your organization.

Though practical experience we have broken our approach to behavior development into a series of steps. All too often leadership teams come together and decide the behaviors needed and speak to them at townhall meetings and, other than some printed materials and posters, nothing really changes. This sequenced approach ensures that the leadership team have time to reflect on the impact of their own behaviors (individually and as a team) on the rest of the organization. It also gives time for the leadership team to learn how to have good purposeful conversation around behavior amongst themselves as a group of peers. This allows the leadership team to practice and build confidence before they bring it to the next level down in the organization and subsequently get input from the wider team. This is where we truly engage in the participative transformation process.

The approach is broken into steps based on the experience our team has had in various organizations. It also creates review and check points to ensure the organization is aligned and moving together. In this process slow is good! You get one chance at doing this right. If it doesn't hit the mark organization muscle memory will kick in in a negative fashion. It will be four to five years before you can look for 'engagement' again in 'another effort' at developing organizational culture. So a slow, purposeful, consistent, and communicative approach is the way to go.

5.6. Developing and Deploying Behaviors one step at a time.

We have summarised the flow of suggested activity in the diagram below.

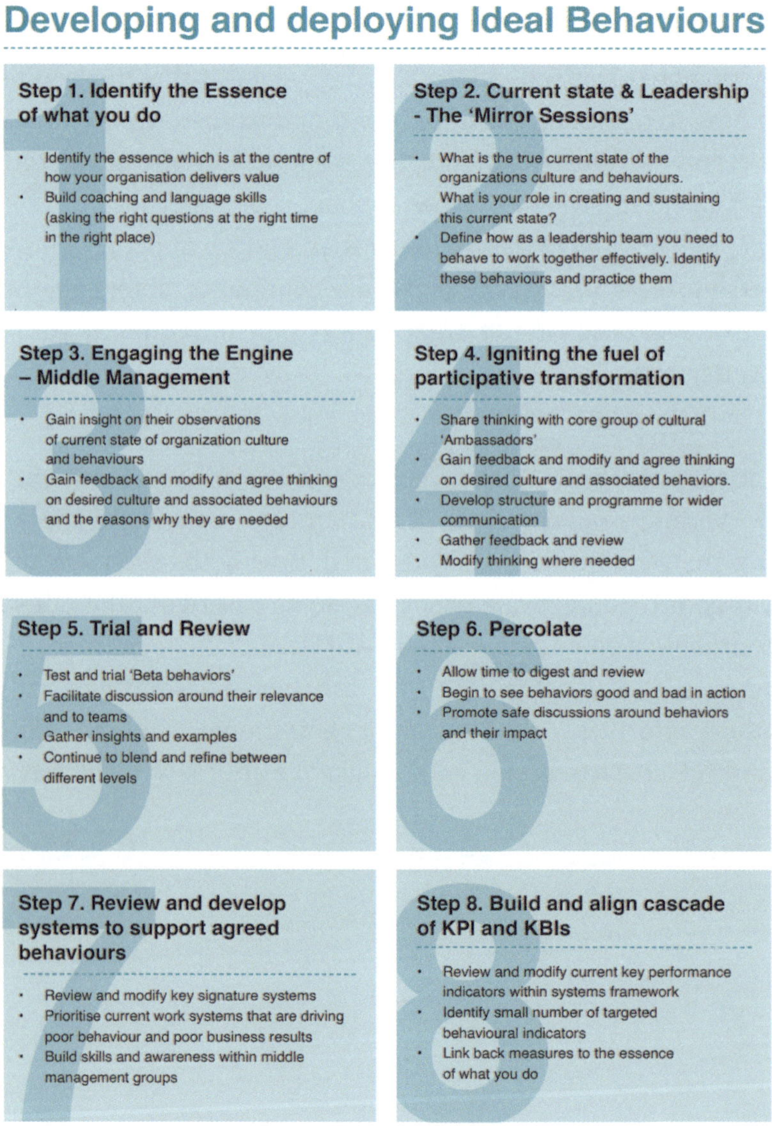

Developing and deploying Ideal Behaviours

Step 1. Identify the Essence of what you do

- Identify the essence which is at the centre of how your organisation delivers value
- Build coaching and language skills (asking the right questions at the right time in the right place)

Step 2. Current state & Leadership - The 'Mirror Sessions'

- What is the true current state of the organizations culture and behaviours. What is your role in creating and sustaining this current state?
- Define how as a leadership team you need to behave to work together effectively. Identify these behaviours and practice them

Step 3. Engaging the Engine – Middle Management

- Gain insight on their observations of current state of organization culture and behaviours
- Gain feedback and modify and agree thinking on desired culture and associated behaviours and the reasons why they are needed

Step 4. Igniting the fuel of participative transformation

- Share thinking with core group of cultural 'Ambassadors'
- Gain feedback and modify and agree thinking on desired culture and associated behaviors.
- Develop structure and programme for wider communication
- Gather feedback and review
- Modify thinking where needed

Step 5. Trial and Review

- Test and trial 'Beta behaviors'
- Facilitate discussion around their relevance and to teams
- Gather insights and examples
- Continue to blend and refine between different levels

Step 6. Percolate

- Allow time to digest and review
- Begin to see behaviors good and bad in action
- Promote safe discussions around behaviors and their impact

Step 7. Review and develop systems to support agreed behaviours

- Review and modify key signature systems
- Prioritise current work systems that are driving poor behaviour and poor business results
- Build skills and awareness within middle management groups

Step 8. Build and align cascade of KPI and KBIs

- Review and modify current key performance indicators within systems framework
- Identify small number of targeted behavioural indicators
- Link back measures to the essence of what you do

Figure 15: Step by step guide to identifying and deploying behaviors in your organization © S A Partners

5.7. The Shingo Model as a guide in developing ideal behaviors.

Often, we may need to back check for alignment between the necessary ideal behaviors and how they fit under our value framework. Corporate values, while they may have good intent, can be too high level and vague. Using the Shingo Enterprise Excellence model is a good place to start if you need some guidance or to broaden your current thoughts on values and principles.

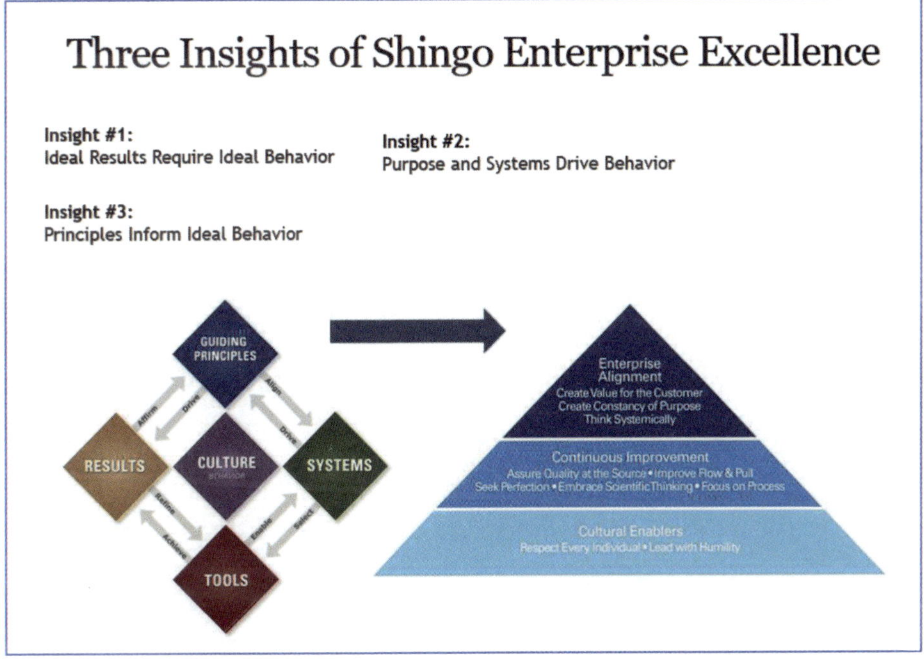

Figure 17: The Shingo Model, Guiding principles and the three insights of Sustainable Enterprise Excellence. (Shingo, 2022)

The Shingo Institute has researched and reviewed global thought leadership in relation to the underlying principles of sustainable enterprise excellence. In a way the institute has done a lot of the 'heavy lifting' for you as regards what excellence means for your organization and what it might look like.

The Shingo Institute provides definitions for each of the principles which are well researched and articulated. However, you still need to translate this into behaviors and statements that are relevant and meaningful to your business and your teams.

Using each of the principles as a lens to examine the organization up we can challenge ourselves with some very searching questions such as:

> If we really lived the principle *'Focus on Process'* in this organization what would that look like?
>
> Do we really understand our processes in the level of detail required to ensure consistent excellent performance and constant improvement?
>
> Do we treat all people in our organization with equal respect and dignity?
>
> Do we listen to and act on the ideas, suggestions, and observations no matter who or where they come from?
>
> Do we give all employees equal opportunity to develop and better themselves?
>
> Do we really seek perfection in the way we approach our work? And if we did, what would we see leaders and managers doing differently?

The exercise is useful as the ten guiding principles help us to highlight gaps in our thinking around observable behaviors. For example, Focus on Process. Ideally it is an observable behavior we need in every organization. But how does it translate to what we do? Usually, we define process by a standard way of doing the work. Hopefully one that is developed by the team engaged directly in the process. The standard while it is a standard is not static. As we learn and understand the details of the process we continue to improve and refine the standard. Focus on process means the relentless learning and standardisation of the way work gets done and how we maintain that standard way of working until a refined and improved process is defined and standardised. If our critical standardized ways of working have not changed and improved in twelve months, then the team and leadership of the area are not focused on process!

Aligning Shingo Enterprise Excellence Principles with existing company values can help find gaps and assist in the interpretation of what these values would look like. Through the activity we should keep challenging ourselves to consider what we would observe happening if any specific value was truly lived in the organization or individual team. There may be some debates as to which principle aligns with what value, but in the end, what we should observe is how we interpret them into actual behaviors.

Please go ahead and download the Shingo Institute's guidebook and definitions of the principles and review the supporting concepts behind the principles and try this exercise for yourself with your team. Better still sign yourself and the team up for a Shingo Discover Excellence introductory workshop!

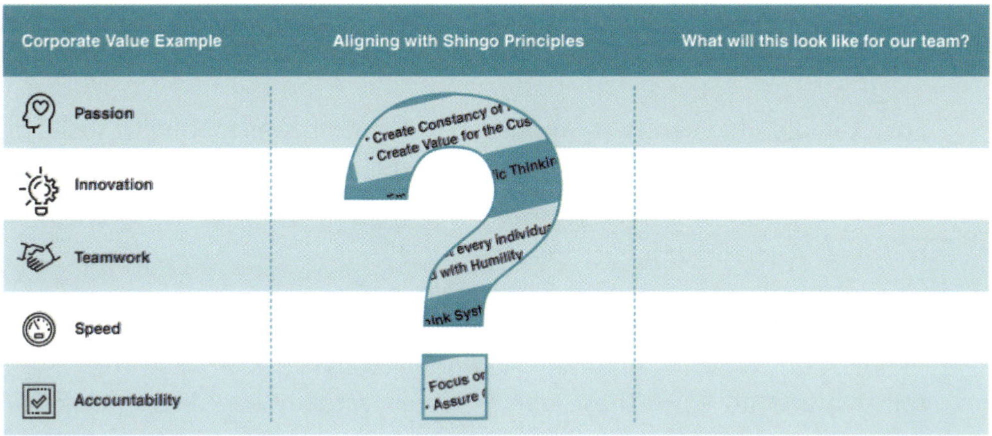

Corporate Value Example	Aligning with Shingo Principles	What will this look like for our team?
Passion		
Innovation		
Teamwork		
Speed		
Accountability		

Figure: 18 Exercise in Aligning Shingo Enterprise Excellence Principles to existing corporate values

Corporate Value Example	Aligning with Shingo Principles	What will this look like for our team?
Passion	· Create Constancy of Purpose · Create Value for the Customer	
Innovation	· Embrace Scientific Thinking · Seek Perfection	
Teamwork	· Respect every individual · Lead with Humility	
Speed	· Think Systemically · Flow and Pull Value	
Accountability	· Focus on Process · Assure Quality at Source	

Figure 19: Define what would actually be observed at various levels of the organization if the Shingo Principle was really 'lived'.

Once we have aligned our values to a source such as the Shingo Guiding Principles, teams can begin to have more detailed and focused discussions around what ideal behaviors would actually look like both at site level and at local department level.

For example, if speed is an important value that is aligned with focus on process, what would focus on process look like in the warehouse or accounting department and why are these behaviors important in relation to speed in serving our customer's needs?

Considering the Shingo Guiding Principles in our attempt to assimilate defined values into an organization allows teams to challenge their thinking around what these values would actually look like in practice. What would we see? What would we hear - if these values and the underlying principles were truly lived?

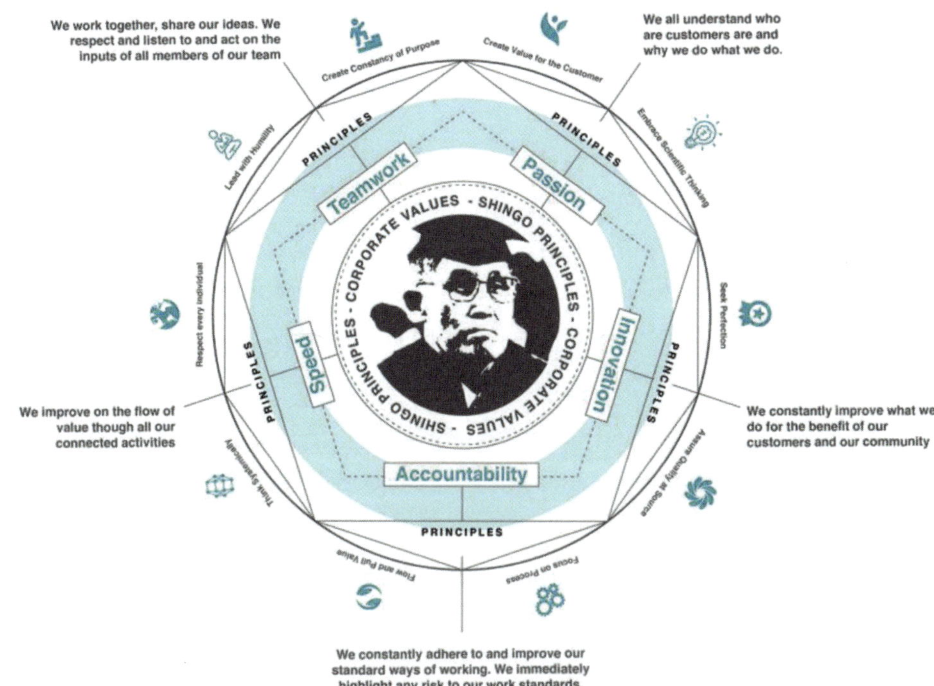

Figure 20: The Shingo Principles and philosophy can help organizations define what the high level values will look and sound like in the workplace.

Using Shingo Enterprise Excellence guiding principles can allow teams to translate sometimes bland high level corporate values into something they can relate to within their organization and in the work that they do.

5.8. *Steps for deploying ideal behaviors*

Step 1 (a) Identify the Essence of what you do as an organization.

Forget the hype. At a basic level what is at the core of how you deliver value to your customers? Or the next step in your supply chain?

Leaving the hype behind can allow you to focus on what most people in your organization do with their time. Where the bulk of people are, tends to be where most of the issues lie. Remember the examples from earlier in chapter two, the farrier, the salesperson.

In some cases, issues may be outside the control of your team. For example, poor supplier quality impacts the ability of the team to do what they need to do well and consistently. *But the team still need to do what they do well and consistently*. If supplier performance is critical how are the observable behaviors in your organization focused on getting the very best performance from your suppliers to ensure your team's success?

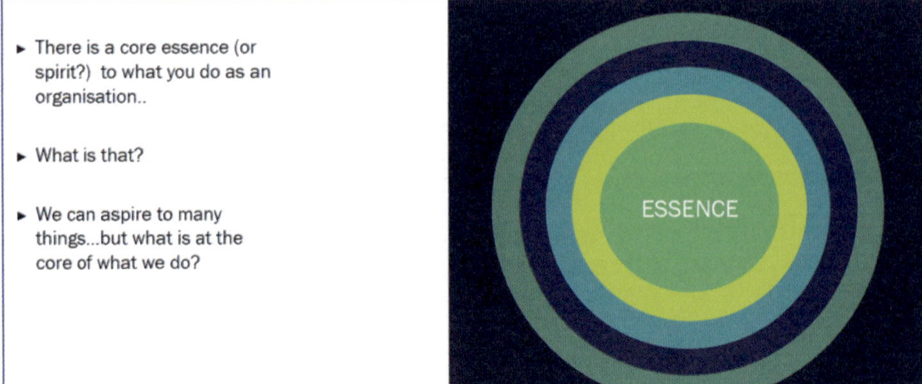

Figure 16: Get clarity on the core of what you do: your essence to add value. © S A Partners.

Step 1 (b) Selecting your value framework

Choose your appropriate value framework and take a current-state view of leadership behaviors.

Don't panic! A value framework is often something you have already. Your values are the principles that should help your organization decide what is right and wrong, and how to act in particular situations. It may be a framework published by your corporation. You might consider guidance from the Shingo Enterprise Excellence Model and its ten guiding principles. Or as a leadership team you may have a set of values that describe how you want the business to 'feel like'. Whatever the source, keep the number of core values to a minimum.

If you are struggling, keep it simple. Here are some questions that may help you focus on some core values:

> What is the culture or feel we want in our organization and why is that important to achieving our results?
>
> Is improvement important to us?
>
> Do we need to keep pace with technology and new skills?
>
> How important is alignment across the organization?
>
> Safety and environmental concerns may be very topical in your business, do we need to express them as a value?
>
> Does your local community play a significant role in what you do, through co-operation re-licencing, recruit source, social responsibility?
>
> Are you working in highly regulated industry?
>
> How important is current scientific research to your business?
>
> Is patient care at the basis of what you do?
>
> How important is it for you to develop the skills of your team?

How close do you <u>really</u> need to be to your customers?

Where a corporate value structure exists, go with it. There is usually some value in the thinking behind it. But you must research it and understand the thinking behind it. However, at the end of the day, it is the actual observed behaviors that are critical to your success as a business that you must focus on as a leadership team. Having values on the wall, key chains or T-shirts is useless unless we see values expressed as an actual behaviour that contributes to the overall success of a business.

Step 2 (a) Leadership Reality – Welcome to the Mirror Sessions & the shadow cast

'Every leader casts a shadow, so be aware of the fact that people will do what you do.' David Novak. Chairman and CEO Yum! Brands.

As a leadership team you are about to start conversations in your organization about values and behaviors. Now is the time as <u>one</u> leadership team to begin to practice your own language and approach to behaviors and values. It is also the time when we hold a mirror up in relation to our own behaviors as leaders working together as peers. How do we work together as a team? Are we aligned? What is our approach to improvement in the work we do together as a team? The team must also consider how our behaviors and leadership are reflected within the wider organization. The shadow we cast as leaders. This is the essence of the Mirror Sessions. In these workshops we carefully but purposefully explore these questions as leaders of this organization.

The shadow of leadership we believe, consists of three elements. The first two elements reflect how leaders are mindful and skilful in their use of language and their listening skills during interactions with their team. How they enquire and probe effectively and listen to the quality of the dialogue around a given subject or issue. It is also how they hold individuals to account effectively without crushing them. This awareness of listening skills and use of language we refer to as acoustic management which we will discuss later.

The third element revolves around prioritization and alignment as a leadership team. Nothing frustrates teams more than conflicting priorities and overburden. Good policy deployment and regular check in conversation by the leadership team members in co-ordinated fashion should avoid this issue. The primary system to enable these check-ins and quality conversations, as we will discuss, is the tiered management system.

If these three elements are in place and working well together in a synchronised way the shadow from the leadership is strong purposeful and engaging. If one element is missing or not in sync with the others, the shadow from the leadership team is weak and confusing.

The mirror sessions allow open conversations around what the leadership team see and hear as not ideal behaviors in the current organization. We often run this as a workshop exercise with each senior leader taking the time to think about and describe the less-than-ideal behaviors they currently observe within the organization. Each leader develops their list and gives some evidence of what they observe and how often it is observed. Each leader must be clear on how the described behaviour negatively impacts bottom line business performance. The team are encouraged to say things as they are, but back statements by observable evidence or available data. This can be a difficult exercise, but with good honest engagement it is a powerful starting point.

The team may talk about

> The number of repeated noncompliance observations or CAPAs.
>
> It could be the level of frantic activity across the site prior to a regulatory audit. It could be the number of heated conversations we see between various groups.
>
> Maybe it is a sense of the number of 'dropped balls' where departments failed to share information in a timely manner.

The better the quality of observations and the more real they are, the better the quality of the next part of the exercise will be.

For the next stage, each leader pairs up with a colleague and shares their thoughts. There will be some common observations and some topics for discussion. After some discussion and alignment, this pair joins with a second pair and carry out the same review. Very quickly the list of less-than-ideal behaviors are gathered into what the leadership believe are commonly observed less than ideal behaviors that have a very real impact on the performance of the business.

Number	Not Ideal observable or audible behaviour	Where does it occur?	Impact on our business performance or reputation Now and in The Future
1			
2			
3			
4			
5			
6			
7			
8			
9			
10			

Figure 21: – Your outputs from discussions on not ideal behaviors in your business today!

The leadership team have had some discussion around their current values framework. Spread out before them is a list of maybe eight to twelve less than ideal behaviors that are known to inhibit the business from performing at its best.

Two difficult questions arise from this exercise:

1. Given that the observed behaviors reflect the behaviors within management, how have or are the leadership team supported or contributing to these less-than-ideal behaviors?
2. How do 'we' as the leadership team behave with each other? What behaviors do we need to change in the way we work together?

This is a very important moment for the team. Often the team need to absorb the thoughts arising from the conversations. During our consulting work we allow the team time to absorb these outputs and the questions above. They return to normal work but with the homework of observing their own interaction with these observable behaviors when they occur during their work week.

Leaders involved with this workshop return to normal work activity with a heightened sense of two things.

1. The impact of behaviors on performance
2. An awareness of how their behaviors can influence the behaviors they observe

The team often regroup after a week or two and a richer more informed conversation ensues. For example, they may have found themselves in the middle of a fire-fighting conversation and realized that rather than facilitating the conversation around the issue their inclination was to own it! They find themselves jumping into solution mode rather that stepping back and looking at the team's approach to problem solving and finding and controlling root cause. They may find themselves in a conversation with a subordinate who complains about the behavior of an individual yet that behavior was left unchallenged.

Step 2 (b) The Leadership pact – We must practice what we intend to preach!

Given that the conversation is going to move to the wider organization about behaviors and culture, what are the necessary behaviors <u>**we**</u> need as **a leadership team** to ensure **we** work effectively and support the wider organization?

Reviewing the list of not ideal behaviors allows the leadership team to create a list of initial organizational 'draft behaviors' that they feel are important and which **they** can sign up to. The team must be prepared to apply these behaviors – or, as we prefer to call them, '*ways of working*' – to themselves initially and hold each other accountable to them. Together they practice as a team in the work that they do together.

One leadership team I worked with admitted that '*too much stuff was not talked about*'. As a team they were not having the '*right conversation*'. One of their adopted behaviors was simply…

> '*Let's ensure we have the right conversations at the right time.*'

So, what did this mean in practice?

> Members of the Leadership team needed to ensure that they had data and facts to support a position. If data or information were not available, the conversation would be suspended until more in-depth information was available.
>
> Uneasy silences were noted and 'poked' to get to the bottom of any concerns.
>
> Unanimous approval and head nodding was followed by the question '*are we sure we all understand the full picture here*?'
>
> If an issue was raised late or in the wrong forum the question was asked.. '*What stopped us talking about or being aware of this when we were in the tier two meeting?*'
>
> At the end of each meeting the question was asked, '*is there anything left unsaid?*'

While visibly awkward at first the leaders soon got into the spirit of why and how important for themselves personally and as a team to ensure the right conversation was happening at the right time. It began to significantly improve communication amongst themselves. It also significantly improves the alignment and prioritisation of activity between departments. There was no space for a misunderstood priority. If priorities were unclear, why did we not have the right conversation?

While these draft behaviors were not deployed to the wider organization, the leadership team soon began to see the impact of their behavioural standards on their own teams. The leadership team met regularly to review and share their learnings and support and coach each other. On occasion a leader might admit that they had not handled a situation with their team the way he or she would have liked to, given the behaviors the team were aspiring to achieve. Through peer-to-peer conversations and coaching the leader could replay conversations and 'practice' a new way asking questions and interacting more effectively with their teams.

Being part of a leadership team can be a lonely and stressful place. It is a fantastic thing to observe a leadership team begin to help and guide each other into a new way of working together. Peer-to-peer support at any level is a powerful force and it will be a subject we will come back to.

Step 3 Focus on the reality of the current state.

At this point we are almost suspending our thoughts on the higher values identified for the business. There is an important reason for this. Organizations often stop once values are identified and begin to publish and communicate them thinking that the organization can now get direction from the values and their definitions. However, we can sometimes push values that are disconnected from the current reality.

We may for example make statements as to the importance of safety. But the reality on the shop floor is that there are lots of safety issues that have been highlighted but not addressed effectively.

We may make statements about respect and the importance of inclusion within our workplace yet there are obvious behaviors among leaders and managers and some teams that do not reflect the value of respect and inclusion.

We may speak to the importance of the customer or patient focus; in reality, the teams know that the processes they work with are broken and are not providing the best outcomes for the customer or patient.

So, we need to be mindful of the true realities and challenges our teams deal with each day as they try to do their job as best they can, given the current reality of doing their work.

At this point, to make the process real and sustainable, we need to engage the wider team in conversations around current state behaviors and culture. Unfortunately, in many situations, enthusiastic leadership teams begin to dive straight down to the shop floor. Talking about and observing good and not so good behaviors, completely bypassing the middle management group. Over-enthusiasm can lead teams straight into the minefield that is *'Leaders Standard Work'*. This is a mistake.

The meat in the sandwich – middle management

We often hear discussion about the "squeezed middle layers". In some bizarre situations all the woes of the business seem to be due to the lack of management and leadership skill or alignment at the middle-management levels. Leadership teams can often refer to a consistent lack of ownership and accountability in this group: *'They just don't seem to be engaged or take ownership for the current state.'*

The middle management teams did not suddenly appear in the organization. The issues or problems and their links to behaviors and perceived poor attitudes again did not suddenly appear. They have developed over time or may have always been there. Now unfortunately they are how the 'work works around here'. If we want to see greater ownership and accountability, we must first create the desire and interest to do so.

To begin to have a real impact on improving the behaviors around our 'ways of working' we need to engage the engine that is the middle management community. We do this in a similar way to the conversation we had earlier with the senior teams. But as we are often dealing with a larger cohort of individuals, we may need to break the activity out after an initial positioning session led by site senior leadership, into smaller working groups.

Be prepared for some difficult conversations. One of the ground rules we put in place for these conversations is we look at process not person. Conversations that have a risk of getting personal are raised back up to a process viewpoint. *'What may be wrong with our process to cause individuals to behave in that way?'*. Through a series of workshops some of which are facilitated by members of the leadership team, another list of not ideal observable behaviors is formed.

By some amazing force of nature, this list is often eighty to ninety percent the same as the list generated by the leadership! However, it is important for the leadership team to listen to and explore the 10-20% differences. These are often the not ideal behaviors that the middle management group observe **within the leadership team**. They may also cover the behaviors that they see at the shop floor. These are often the critical conversations that allow the teams to gain trust in the entire process.

Don't be afraid to explore the difficult issues. Remember process focus.

> Why is it that people feel ill informed? We have not clearly laid out how we communicate important information to all levels. (Emails on noticeboards do not work, trust me!)
>
> Why is there a lack of trust with leadership? Priorities keep changing. The process of aligning and reviewing priorities is either non-existent or not adequate. We see actions that are at odds with the messaging from the leadership team.
>
> People do not feel engaged, their opinions are not heard! – We had a process for regular one to one sessions and to meet with area leads but this habit has fallen away when we got busier!

Once we are honest and genuine in our interest and efforts to improve the way we all need to work together, teams will listen. But the conversations need to be real. If the current environment is tense and difficult, we strongly recommend professional facilitation for these working sessions. A facilitator can set ground rules and keep conversations away from personal attacks and finger pointing. A facilitation can keep bringing the conversation back to the bigger picture and ensure that the team remains grounded and focused on this.

We also recommend we keep the conversation around behaviors at a high level. Try not to get sucked into *'we are always late for meetings'*. We see a lot of sad dusty looking meeting clocks with red zones for meeting time adherence, with flat batteries. Better to ask, 'why do we need so many meetings to make a decision?' *What would allow us to trust those closest to the work to make the right decision at the right time?'*

Again, with the middle management group, we allow time to practice and reflect on the behaviors we would like to see within the middle management group. Also, we draw out the necessary behaviors between the middle management and the leadership team. The team agree to commit and practice but give themselves the space to make mistakes. It will be a journey and a learning process. Over time both the leadership and middle management team can share their observations and mistakes.

It is a wonderful thing to hear a management team member recount a conversation he or she had with either a peer in the room or with one of their direct reports. The conversation may not have gone well. The expressed behaviors leading to or resulting from the interaction were not ideal. In the safe environment of peer to peer coaching the individual is asked, *'So how would you have done if differently?' 'What is the conversation you would have now?'* Like a reset function in a video game, the individual resets the scene and practices having a different conversation in front of their peers. This is a massively powerful learning environment. Most of the observers have been in or could be in the very same situation.

> **To support the behaviors we aspire to in an organization, we need to create supportive environments for leaders and managers to practice having the right conversations.**

Step 4 – Igniting the fuel of participative transformation

The phrase ***'power to the people'*** is very relevant to the process of deploying behaviour into an organization. When it is done well, we are ceding power to every individual in our organization. We are allowing them to call out activities or actions that are outside of the agreed behaviors or agreed ways of working that **they** have decided are necessary for the organization to succeed as one organization. Wow! Imagine that situation happening every day at every level of the organization. That's transformative participation in action.

It is not as if we are seeing red cards given out or people telling tales. It is as simple as this. In one organization one of the ways of working (WOWs) that the team agreed on was, *'let us always assume positive intent'*. In a story told within one of the working groups a supervisor recounted a situation where they were busy at their desk. The phone rang. From the number of the phone the supervisor knew it was one of the planners. The supervisor's initial thought was *'I'm up to my neck here and I don't need this conversation'*. But they reflected on the behaviour *'let's always assume positive intent'*. The supervisor appreciated that their colleague was also trying to do their job as best they could and probably needed some piece of information. The supervisor took the call and had a good collegiate conversation with their planner colleague. In the supervisor's mind the *'Planner'* became a *'Colleague'* who was working to help ensure we all achieve what we needed to achieve.

What if the supervisor had not taken the call? Maybe a piece of information may have been missed or forgotten? In two weeks' time the organization could well have been dealing with a problem associated with that missed piece of information.

Getting back to the equestrian analogy: for want of a nail the shoe was lost. For want of a shoe the horse was lost etc! Just as the accumulation of less-than-ideal behaviors give rise to poor inconsistent performance. The accumulation of the constant expression of ideal behaviors helps move the organization towards more consistent enterprise-wide levels of deep excellence.

Step 5 - Deploying behaviors into the organization -Trial and review

To release the power with the wider organization we need again to engage in honest open dialogue about the current state reality. The organization cannot tell or create expectations around how people should behave. Rather we start the conversations from the question:

> *'What needs to work really well in your area to allow you and your team do the work your need to do really well?'*

In asking this question the organization is acknowledging that it cannot tell individuals how to behave. This is an adult to child conversation. There are obvious exceptions here where there are clear breaches of standards or safety protocols. But even in these extreme situations, the enquiry is around why did this situation occur in the first place. What drove an individual to take a short cut on safety procedures?

So, while telling people how to behave is not ideal, we can open discussions around the behaviors that are needed to get the work done in the safest most 'hassle free' way.

To begin to deploy into the wider employee groups we need to create enviroments where individual team members can have good open conversations about current state culture and behaviors.

The organization can facilitate this by seeking volunteers (behavior ambassadors) from across the organization to participate in the process. We estimate that for every hundred employees you will need five ambassadors. These individuals will, after some initial training and conversations with the leadership team, take responsibility for hosting working sessions with small groups of their colleagues. It is within these smaller groups open safe environments are created to discuss current state culture and behaviors. The ambassadors will also prompt discussions around what behavior is needed to support people in doing their work effectively.

This information is gathered confidentially with no names attributed to any statements. Ambassadors will gather and collate feedback into core themes by comparing their notes from their individual workshops. These review sessions are ideally supported by members of the leadership team.

The ambassadors will subsequently meet with the leadership team to feedback progress and recurring behavioral themes within the current state.

Once the ambassadors have completed their workshops and complied the common current state themes and gathered thoughts on ideal behaviors, the ambassadors present the information to both the senior leadership and the middle management team members. This 'blending session' allows a critical mass of individuals within the organization to gain alignment on what the current state culture and behaviour is really like and what ideal behaviors are necessary for the organization to succeed as one team.

Once again these are powerful sessions which can start a real movement for change in the organization. But the danger is we have this communication and alignment session gather some ideal behaviors, communicate them and job done!

Nope. This does not work. We have only begun to move the 'water wheel'. It will need a constant flow to maintain its momentum.

Step 6 - Percolation

The blending session should provide the organization with some initial guideline high level values. These should still be considered in development or 'Beta Values'. This ensures that the door remains open for further development. The blending session will also provide examples of how these values translate into observable behaviors at various levels and across different departments.

But again, it would be dangerous to just run with these values without getting feedback from the wider community in the business. We call this percolation!

The initial beta values and example behaviors are fed back into the business either through existing meeting structures (tiered boards) or dedicated short discussion huddles. The 'beta values and behaviors' are posted in work areas and supervisors and managers take **dedicated time** with their teams to discuss them and ensure alignment and agreement. Again there is a role to be played here by the senior leadership team and senior leaders drop into these discussion to listen and, where appropriate, contribute to the conversations.

The period for feedback is defined: maybe three-four weeks, to ensure all shift structures can be included in the conversations.

It is interesting how often valuable insights are raised around culture and behaviors even at this late stage in the process. If this is the case, it is a real sign that the process is building trust and the organization is beginning to take ownership for their agreed behaviors or ways of working together.

Step 7 - Reviewing systems and the behaviors they should support

In chapter six we will discuss core system or signature system and their critical role in support the behaviors and culture in the business. We know that some systems, either through vagueness, complexity, heritage, or the measures within them, may not support the necessary behaviors we need to succeed. Instead, they may facilitate error, they may force workarounds, they may drive departments to work against each other and they may foster a compliant rather than a committed culture with the business. All of these we will explore in the subsequent chapter.

Suffice to say that the performance measures and indicators we discover during this process of deployment must find a home where they are visible, reviewed, and improved. High level measures of culture and behaviour must be visible at high level senior management tier board or scorecard reviews. There must be an acceptance and understanding at this level that the lagging measures we spend so much time and discussions on are an outcome of the behaviors and culture which up to now have been given only tacit attention – if at all.

Likewise, at each level of the business the behaviors should begin to appear within key signature systems. How are the improvement projects and ideas aligned to business need? How do I see these in each department? How do I review the role the supervisor and managers have in supporting focused improvement and problem solving in their areas of responsibility? Is this part of their annual appraisal or bonus process?

In the maintenance area how do the maintenance team review and assess their customer value criteria? How do they see and measure flow? The same goes for the quality control department.

To ensure the sustainment and improvement of the work completed during this deployment process, we must review and refine the core systems in the business to give voice and visibility to the ideal behaviors. Are they being expressed as Key Behavioural Indicators KBIs and how can we improve or change them if they no longer apply?

Step 8 - measure and refine -sustaining the momentum - finding the illusive KBIs

Now that the organization has aligned on cultural values and has considered ideal behaviors how do we sustain this focus?

The leadership team must now consider how to measure these behaviors and their real impact on the business? The important point here is real business impact. Too often we can create measures on behaviors but fail to make the connection to the real business impact.

> *We generate ideas* – but do we see real improvement of cost or lead times
>
> *We recognise effort* – but for what? Do we see staff turnover reduce or better process performance?

We have safety conversations – but are the level of accidents and near misses and risk levels really reducing?

Promote customer focus – have our complaints reduced and sales increased? How do we understand, review and improve our internal customer needs?

We measure the number of A3 problem solving sheets – but do we see a reduction in CAPAs or recurring issues?

We must make the link between what we agree are our values and the resulting ideal behaviors and the overall performance of our site.

Our colleague Ken Wisinski and Colin Scott have some useful tips on developing Key Behavioral indicators.

KBIs should be developed within the local team and should be based on behaviors needed to make the team and/or work more effective and improve the results. They are NOT the type of measure that can be easily copied from another team or situation.

In a perfect world, selected KBIs would describe <u>ideal</u> behavior. Realistically, KBIs that are needed in a specific team at a given time, may not necessarily represent ideal. Start small. Strive for something that can be easily measured (simple is better) and will begin to drive the team towards ideal behavior.

KBIs are best when inwardly directed. The focus should be how you or your team can behave to improve effectiveness and results. When specific behavior is needed from others (people outside the immediate team), it must be influenced by YOUR behavior. Behavior begets behavior!

KBIs may become stale. Over time, the desired behavior hopefully becomes a regular habit and no longer needs reinforcement & recognition through an indicator. When that happens, the behavior (and associated KBI) should be modified to move the team ever closer to ideal.

Practical tips on KBIs from Colin and Ken. © S A Partners.

The table below outlines an example of how to align behaviors to key business performance.

Lagging KPI	Leading Process Measures	Leading Behavioural Indicators
Average cost per unit produced	Yield Scrap OEE	Department reporting and acting on.. On Time In Full (OTIF) issues. Focused productivity ideas generated and implemented Leaders Gemba
Average Co2 consumption per unit produced	Equipment Idle Time Scrap, Yield	Department standard work reviews completed Focused energy ideas generated and implemented Leaders Gemba. Pre-identified equipment powered down when not required by team members
Leadtime to DC **OTIF**	Adherence to plan Process Leadtime	Adherence to departmental plan Process lead time adherence Huddle board Kata reviews Workplace Organization Flow system review Leader Gemba
Lost Time Accidents	Good catch Tool box talks	Process safety walks completed OTIF Focused safety suggestion generated and implemented Quarterly safety Risk Prevention Number RPN reduction Leader Gemba
Staff Turn Over	Staff Development targets. Recognition, Community Support. Employee survey Qtrly	Leader's coaching schedule adherence Leader 360 feedback PDPs completed on time and to standard Number of recognitions aligned to site goals and agreed behaviors. Employee engagement with charitable activity number of events and number of volunteers Huddle board/meeting Kata reviews Senior Leaders Gemba
Compliance	Process Leadtime Recurring CAPA	Quarterly Quality Risk Prevention Number RPN reduction Recurring CAPAs, CAPA effective closure Open A3 Problem solving Huddle board/meeting Kata reviews Leader Gemba
Customer Complaints	Recurring CAPA OEE Shipping errors Customer	Quarterly Quality Risk Prevention Number RPN reduction Recurring CAPAs, CAPA effective closure Open A3 Problem solving Huddle board/meeting Kata reviews Customer reviews and visits Leaders schedule customer visit

Figure 22: Lagging KPIs and their leading KBIs © S A Partners

I often use the example of an elite athlete such as a high jumper to help teams consider the link between Key Performance Indicators, process indicators and behavioral indicators.

Figure 23: Champion athletes do not just appear. There are systems, processes and behaviors that lead to excellence

Question: So, what is the critical KPI for a high jumper?

Answer: The height of the bar or the number of times they get over the bar.

Question: Are these KPIs Leading or Lagging indicators?

Answer: Lagging

Question: So, what would be some leading process indicators that indicate if the athlete will make it over the bar?

Answer: Speed of approach, position of takeoff. Degree of lateral lean as athlete approaches jump.

Question: So, what would be some important behaviors from the athlete to ensure these leading process indicators can be achieved?

Answers:

Does the athlete turn up for team training, on time and prepared?

Do they willingly help train other junior members of the team? (Thereby helping themselves learn).

Do they stick rigidly to their diet?

Do they watch and observe competitors' performance and style?

Do they learn more about the science of what they do, physiology, nutrition, resilience mindset?

Do they share this knowledge with the team to improve teams' overall performance?

Do they give themselves time to prepare mentally before an event?

All the above are observable behaviors some of which could be measured if we so wish. However, if these behaviors are not expressed by the athlete, it is unlikely that the 'process indicators' will be achieved consistently resulting in inconsistent or generally poor performance in elite competition.

Companies often struggle to identify key behavioural indicators limiting them to suggestions and safety observations. While these are indeed behavioural indicators, we also must ensure the alignment with organizational goals and whether they are implemented! It is also vital to ensure that these KBIs are more a reflection of the quality of supervisors, managers and leadership rather than a lack of engagement from the teams!

We need KBIs to be aligned to what is important to us. It is strange that many businesses measure lots of metrics but yet fail to see the indications of behaviour and culture behind the metric. If all our Corrective and Preventative Actions (CAPAs) are closed out in the last few days before they are due, what does that tell us about our behaviour towards problems solving? Equally when we see the same or nearly the same CAPAs occurring? An example might be raising CAPAs repeatedly for document errors that are put down to root cause as operator attentiveness, mistake, or lack of training. The metric should speak more to the quality and complexity of our work design and documentation rather than the quality and capability of our colleagues.

If we continue to change the production schedule due to the availability or quality of raw material or the availability of skilled labour what organizational behaviors does that metric speak to?

I have come across situations where supervisors will preferentially select work that will earn more hours financially for their department rather than work to the planned schedule. Equally I have come across planners who plan with little grasp of product changeover restrictions and no direct demand from the customer. Do these examples speak to behaviors?

There are many metrics in our business that at first glance are considered KPIs but have a strong underlying behavioral element. Teasing these out allows us to drive conversations at local department level in every area of our business. If we want to encourage change and improvement yet it takes us three months to get a revised document signed off, then how will a culture of improvement be sustained?

So, what are the behaviors we could observe around document change? Do we require multiple signatures from people who do not understand the process? Will managers and supervisors leave their documentation change review to a Friday evening? When documents enter the document update department are they treated based on priority or FIFO? Or are they batched until someone is available to review them and get them on the system? Or is there a constant process of expediting 'urgent' document update due a pending audit or CAPA close date?

All of these situations give us indications of what behaviors could be observed and possibly measured within different local elements of the document change process.

The beauty is that we should not dictate any of these measures to the individuals and teams involved in process improvement and document update. We could simply state that FLOW is one of the key values in our business and ask two questions.

> What are the key things that need to happen to ensure we get flow in our process improvement and document change activity?
>
> What are the things we should keep an eye on (measure) and where should we look for these?

Very quickly the team will define what needs to be measured and where. These measures can then form part of any tier meeting or department huddle. If they are not having the desired impact, then maybe we need to review as a team and find different measures to ensure flow in our process improvement and document change activity.

The final element of the sustaining process comes back around to the actions, engagement and presence of the leadership community, and the shadow they cast into the organization which we will discuss in the next chapter.

5.9. Pulling it together

When an organization embarks on a culture change initiative it must be based on three core realities:

> **What are the core elements of our ability to provide value to our customers?**
>
> **Do we understand the behaviors we need expressed in our teams which allow us to provide this value in the most effective and efficient way possible?**
>
> **What is the true picture of where we are now, both in terms of performance and culture?**

Unless leadership teams can have real open discussions around these three questions there is no point in moving forward.

Sustainable cultural transformation towards levels of Deep Excellence require a different way of looking at engagement. We use the term transformative participation to describe an environment where every person understands at a very personal level what the organization is trying to achieve and what are the base values that the organization stands for. Power in effect is ceded to majority of the workforce to manage and ensure that the culture and behaviors they have agreed are necessary to support these values and objectives are in place and are upheld. The team want to be part of the story of the organization.

While power to manage culture is ceded to frontline teams, senior leaders and middle managers must constantly check in and actively support the desired culture through the purposeful design and management of key signature systems within the business. These work systems, enterprise systems, and leadership systems are core to supporting and enabling the desired culture and behaviors. In the following chapter we will discuss these systems and the systems architecture behind them.

6 Systems: the architecture of deep excellence

6.1. Systems: the architecture of deep excellence

> 'In spite of the fact that management is responsible for the system, or for lack of the system, I find in my experience that few people in industry know what constitutes a system.'
>
> W. Edwards Deming

If you want to learn something new read an old book, said a wise man once. It is scary and often depressing to realise how true this statement is. Especially if you are a management consultant!

When we read about the contributions by Deming in the eighties and nineties to true quality and productivity effectiveness, we can only wonder, what if? What if every organization really grasped what Deming was putting forward in relation to quality output and people's engagement with the work that they do? How much more efficient, effective, and harmonious could workplaces be today almost fifty years later?

It is incredible to think that there are organizations operating today running processes at efficiency levels below fifteen percent! This low level of performance can only be maintained by the exorbitant profits achievable within certain sectors. One can only wonder how much more benefit these organizations could bring to civilisation if they could run their businesses at, say, sixty or even eighty percent efficiency? How much waste would be prevented? How much energy could be saved? Is the acceptance of these low levels of efficiency a vestige of some deep tribal element of our stone age brain that might be holding us back for such noble and altruistic type of thinking? As long as our tribe is doing OK, that's all that matters.

6.2. Systems around us

As young boy I was fascinated by the natural world, in particular the ocean. This ultimately led me to a master's degree in oceanography. My research involved the review of the way in which heavy metals from man's industrial and domestic activity could be traced through the sediments, water column and organisms of our oceans. My studies involved trips to the Artic circle the east coast of the United States and the West and East coasts of Ireland and the United Kingdom.

Figure 24: The author John Quirke sampling sediments (some time ago!) off East Coast of the United States.

My work with metal chemistry led me to a role in an electronics company where I developed and managed Electroplating and Ink Manufacturing processes. I stayed in the manufacturing field finally ending up in medical device and pharmaceutical environments and from there into the world of consulting.

But my studies and work in oceanography have always stayed with me. As I progressed in my career two things became clear. Industry did not optimize its processes to minimise the use of precious resources, thereby creating a lot of waste. This waste would eventually end up in some part of our natural environment where its impacts would be studied by another research student!

Secondly, business did not work with an integrated systems mindset. Even as a young fresh engineer it was clear that organizations were not set up to optimise the way important elements of the business worked together for the benefit of the whole.

My studies in oceanography revealed the web of integrated natural systems that have been in place for millennia. I could find traces of copper, lead and zinc which had originated from man's land-based activity in the deepest ocean sediments. These contaminants were carried there through the crossover between living biological systems, and the physical, circulatory and sedimentation systems of our great oceans.

James Lovelock, author of the Gaia hypothesis, showed just how interdependent and finely tuned our natural planetary systems are. During his research in the nineteen eighties, he describes how tiny marine plants called phytoplankton release the gas dimethylsulphide (DMS) which, when it oxidises in the upper atmosphere is a major source of cloud-condensation nuclei (CCN). Thus, where there is an abundance of plankton the presence of DMS and resulting CCN cause clouds to form, reducing light levels and supressing excessive plankton growth (Charlson, Lovelock, Andreae, & Warren, 1987).

Now, all too late, our stone age brain is realising the power of interconnected natural systems to control and regulate our life support unit, planet earth.

Within business we must begin to grasp the idea of integrated systems to ensure our businesses work as effectively and efficiently as possible. Only businesses have the ingenuity and resources to react at the speeds necessary to mitigate the oncoming challenges to our planet. An integrated systems-based approach is critical to allow us to move out of our stone age brain and strive for a business environment that reflects deep excellence.

We need to find better ways to review, manage and improve the way our businesses work both internally and externally. As mentioned earlier there is now a pressing moral obligation on every leadership team to ensure they are utilising the resources made available to them in the most effective and efficient way possible. In addition, leaders must constantly encourage their team to seek out new and better ways to minimize the use of resources and the organization's overall impact on the environment. To run an organization any other way is against the new nature of business.

This wider integrated approach can only be achieved through a systems-based philosophy focused on the way organizations are designed, managed and constantly improved. However, as we will explain later, it is far more than an awareness of individual system structure. The true power of a systems-based philosophy is the integration between these business systems, and how the systems themselves and the integration between them is constantly improved to support the necessary culture and behaviors within the organization.

6.3. *Systems thinking in your business*

In the early nineties Dr W. Edwards Deming raised the importance of systems thinking. He defined a system as..

> a network of interdependent components that work together to try to accomplish the aim of the system. The aim of the system must be clear to everyone in the system.
>
> (Deming W. E., 1993).

He stated that the aim of the system must: (a) be clear for everyone in the system; (b) include plans for the future; (c) be a value judgment; and (d) be defined in terms of activity or methods.

The system itself must undergo iterations of continuous improvement by grasping the knowledge and experience of those working in the system.

'Use of the flow diagram provides a feedback loop for continual improvement of product or service, and continual learning' (Deming W. E., 1993, p. 59). After preparing employees to become lifelong learners, they will constantly scan 'the environment (technical, social, economic) to perceive need for innovation, new product, new service, or innovation of method. A company can to some extent govern its own future' (Deming W. E., 1993, p. 55). By driving the focus on system-based improvement, 'the individual components of the system, instead of being competitive, will by optimization reinforce each other for accomplishment of the aim of the system' (Deming W. E., 1993).

One of the most influential papers I have every read is Deming's 'System of Profound Knowledge'. In this paper Deming sets out a manifesto outlining how business could truly engage with its employees to understand and grasp opportunities to improve their individual work elements to benefit the overall system performance – and in doing so improve the overall performance of the business. In his articles he railed against the top-down management style dominant at the time and all too common today.

Profound Knowledge is: '(1) appreciation for a system; (2) knowledge about variation; (3) theory of knowledge; and (4) psychology' (Deming W. E., 1993, p. xi).

> The aim of a system of profound knowledge is to transform the prevailing style of management. Improving systems through which work is done, not changing the workers, holds the greatest potential for eliminating mistakes. One can use the rule of thumb that 85% of problems are correctable only through changing the systems (under management control) leaving only 15% of the problems for workers to control. Widespread recognition that systems create the majority of the problems should end the blaming of workers. It is at this point that workers will be encouraged to seek out the true systemic sources of problems and correct them.

We can use the analogy of our neural network to describe how the various systems integrate. The optic nerve controls the eye. The vagus nerve the stomach; the various nerves that sense touch, taste, heat. None of these systems can work alone. They integrate with other important systems such as our muscles, our digestive system, our brain through our nervous system via key junction points called nodes.

Defined and structured business systems are in many ways the neural networks of a business. They define how information flows and how work gets done. They intertwine, overlap and are interdependent, just like the mega systems in our natural world.

Forcing ourselves into a systems-based mind set is a critical step in moving out of our stone age brain! We must begin to focus on the big picture and appreciate and manage the critical systems in our business that support the way our teams must work together to achieve our aim.

6.4. So, what is a system?

Let's then consider the systems in your business. First off, we are not talking about your computer or IT or Electronic Resource Planning (ERP) system. By systems in this context, we are referring to the systems by which you achieve the key outcomes of your business.

How you make stuff or provide a service

How you market and sell your offer to your customers to win more business

How you find, develop and maintain talent in your business

How you maintain and optimise the assets, that produce the products and services your customers look for

How you develop talent and skills within your teams

How you align everyone in your business to the purpose and vision of the business

How you develop and deliver new products and services

How you improve what you do

The way you develop leaders to lead teams

Where would you draw the nodes of connectedness between these systems? How well does information between these systems currently flow? What would the monitoring and feedback systems tell us about these systems and whether they are working harmoniously to give purposeful 'life' to our organization?

These are all key fundamental questions we need to consider when organization begin to grasp a systems thinking mindset.

6.5. *Systems thinking and Shingo Institute*

'An organization moves closer to excellence as it achieves its desired results as an outcome of behaviors, driven by systems that can sustain not only the results but also the culture that created them.'

-The Shingo Institute.

In recent years the Shingo institute has consolidated its teaching on the structure of critical business systems. The Shingo institute has constantly focused on the need for organizations to identify ideal behaviors and culture needed for sustainable levels of enterprise excellence. The institute also stresses the need to reflect on the influence of business systems in either enabling or disabling ideal behaviors.

The institute's more recent detailed focus on defining systems structure is welcome. The institute describes systems in three broad groups. Management systems, Work Systems, and Improvement System. Allen and Bosworth in their book, *Systems Design. Building Systems that Drive Ideal Behaviors,* describe the focus and importance of the focus on Work Systems.

Figure 25: System framework from the Shingo Institute

> Of the three types of systems, the work system is the most fundamental. A work system has an internal focus, meaning that it focuses on everything that is needed for an output, i.e., the work being done to provide value to the customer.
>
> The improvement system focuses across the entire organization and through all the departments within the organization. In this way, the systems support building an improvement culture that involves everyone in the organization, everywhere in the organization, all the time.
>
> The focus of the management system is leading the organization by developing system leaders. The purpose of management systems should be to build alignment in the organization around the common purpose and to create value for the customers. However, these purposes are accomplished by the work systems, as supported by the improvement system. Through developing system leaders, the management system assures the work is done, and that continuous improvement is happening throughout the entire organization.
>
> (Allen & Bosworth, 2022)

While we can think of many systems in a given business, the grouping of systems into these broad groups helps organizations to consolidate their thinking around systems in an organization and where existing systems fit within this model. In doing so organizations can begin to gain more control over the design, control and ability of business systems to drive ideal behavior.

When formalizing the focus on systems, it is important to begin with a high-level systems framework. This framework sets out the necessary and expected interactions between systems and ensures alignment to the common purpose of the organization. Expectations on the connections, the gives and the gets, between systems should be clear. We could consider this as the focus on internal customer relationships between given systems in the business. These expectations should be measured and visible with efforts made to constantly improve the overall ability of the system to contribute to the common purpose of the organization.

The systems framework gives leaders a high-level picture of how the organization is structured and aligned to ensure the sustainable and effective delivery of the overall purpose of the organization. Silo thinking is routed out, the focus is on the impact of the whole, not the performance of an individual system.

6.6. Standard structures within a system.

The Shingo Institute describes how each system – no matter which group –should have five essential tools: Standard Work, Reports, Feedback, Schedules and Improvement Log.

Standard Work:

All activity within an organization should be based on a standard: one agreed best way of doing the work. The activities within a business system are no different. Standard work may relate to defined meeting agendas reporting templates. Information sources used to gather data and define how that data is presented. Standard work is the basis for learning and improvement. Each system should define the elements of standard work within it.

Reports:

Each system should provide usable data and information on the systems itself and how it is performing. The reports and how they are compiled should form part of the standard work within the system. The quality and information contained within the reports should be regularly reviewed with the users of the information to ensure it meets their needs. Any improvement to report, structure or contact will be captured as part of the process of improving the system.

Feedback:

Feedback consists of verbal or written communication around various aspects of the system itself. The standard work within the system; the quality of data and reports. the ability of the system in supporting ideal behavior. Feedback must be actively sought and gathered to ensure the system is meeting its stated aim.

Schedules:

Schedules are the cadence of activity within the system. When and where structured meeting and communications take place. When reports are issued. When improvement activity is facilitated, and standard work elements are reviewed. Define schedules enabling the checking and acting element of the overall systems' performance.

Improvement Log

We tend to think of improvement as focusing on work. But here improvement is focused on the system itself. When we sought feedback did that feedback include opportunities to improve? As we learn more about the system and its impacts the standard work within the system needs to be updated to capture that improvement. All of these improvements are a learning activity and demonstrate a commitment to continuous improvement. Improvements are captured, assigned and tracked to completion within the improvement log of the system.

In effect the tools within a system are the way individuals actively and consistently interact with the system. They are the key to allowing the desired behaviors to be expressed within the system. Tools must, therefore, be designed for and with the user. Elegance, simplicity, and relevance are key in the design of system tools.

If the way I report performance is overly complicated, in time, I will not interact with it effectively.

> If I do not get regular feedback on my efforts in a way that relates to me, I will lose interest.

Tools must be designed with the end user in mind and be applicable to the day and night shift teams, fixed and mobile work colleagues. They should be designed to consider the multicultural aspects of our modern workplaces. I have seen great efforts made to develop beautiful standard work procedures in English, but the teams who use them speak Polish Spanish and Portuguese as their first language! The company will argue, but English is our business language. It is for managers maybe, but not at the shop floor where the behaviors we need have real impact.

We talk of respect but in reality we don't show it by ignoring individual capability and needs of our colleagues as regards language.

In effect the use of tools that support a system represent some of the ideal we seek in action. The use of a problem solving tool. How teams fill out data to visualise performance. The selection and recognition of a colleague. Attending and being prepared for a standard meeting. All of these are examples of a situation where a tool is applied to enable a system to support ideal behaviours.

When we review the effectiveness of the system we should always include a review of the tools that allow individuals to interact with the system.

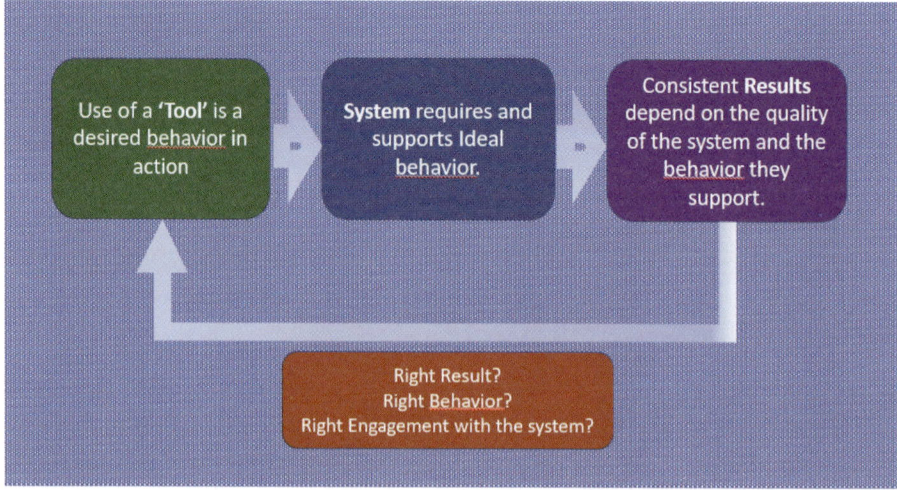

Tools are the human interface with organizational systems. © S A Partners

6.7. *Where to start*

While the sorting of current systems into three broad groups is useful, it can still be overwhelming for organizations to decide where to start. To help with this in our consulting practice we encourage organizations to focus on what we refer to in S A Partners as signature systems. These systems are generally present in every organization in some form, and they are critical to enable all other transformation activity.

These are:

Strategy Deployment

The system by which we deploy strategy and align and engage the organization in our purpose and journey. This will include how that strategy is communicated, cascaded and measured in all parts of the business through the team's alignment and awareness of the organization's Critical Success Factors.

Key work system(s)

This may be a system that is currently performing poorly or is ill-defined currently which poses a risk of compliance or performance issues in the future. It could mean a focus on a particular manufacturing value stream. It could be that current work systems are overly complex resulting in frequent mistakes and rework. It could be the organization selling activity that needs a revamp. Whichever systems we focus on, we will initially keep it to a maximum of two. As the organization learns and gain confidence more work systems can be tackled but, initially, focus and prioritisation is key.

The Improvement system

The focus on the improvement system is more than just doing improvement projects. Instead, it is capturing how the process of improvement works within the entire organization. This system may be managed by the continuous improvement lead, but they do not own it. It should be owned by the site leader. They create expectations on the aim of the system and the role senior leaders play within the system of improvement. The improvement system defines how activity is prioritised and aligned to the strategy of the business. It defines the improvement sub systems, problem solving, total productive manufacturing, workplace organization, tiered management, ideas and suggestions etc and where they fit, and the standard work and review activity associated with each.

Leadership System

The system by which we develop leaders to manage and deploy the culture and behaviors that are critical for the business' long-term sustainable success. Recognizing leadership activity as a system is in itself a real step forward in the journey to deep excellence. By leaders we mean senior leadership, middle management and supervisors. All these levels of leadership have a vital role to play in ensuring work systems and improvement systems are implemented as designed and are supporting the necessary culture and behaviors needed for sustainable excellence.

The focus on developing leaders in the business requires the development of self-leadership, self-awareness, coaching skills, resilience, and the skilful use of dialogue to ensure the right questions are being asked the right way at the right time. We will review this fascinating area of leadership development in the next chapter.

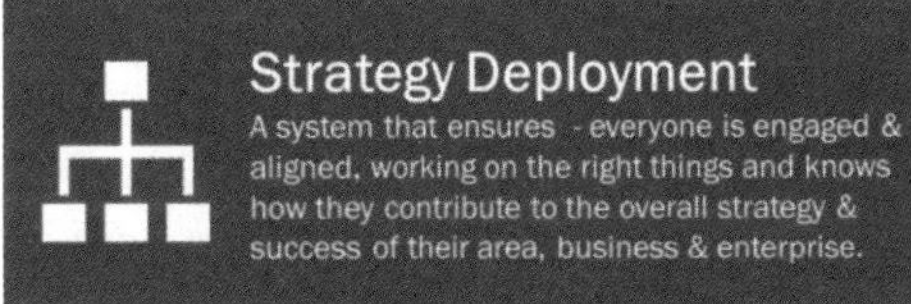

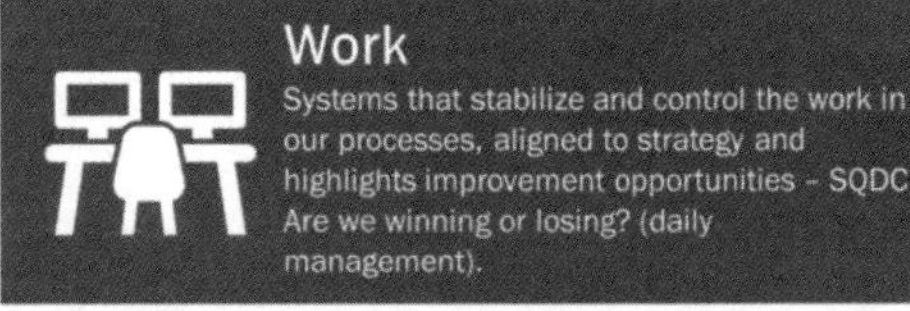

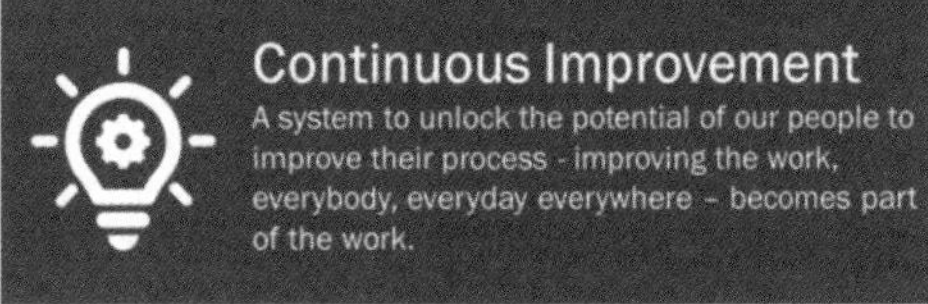

Figure 26: Signature systems – a starting point for systems thinking in your organization. © S A Partners.

As the organization begins to focus on these signature systems, the thinking becomes much more structured and its design more purposeful.

How would we describe the aim of the systems?

What are the behaviors we want the system to support within the organization?

What might be some of the critical workflows or processes within them?

Who owns the overall system and who are the owners of the workflows within the systems?

How and what do we need to measure to review the effectiveness of the system itself?

How do we gather information to continually improve the system itself?

How do we ensure that the activities within each system are fully aligned to the overall purpose of the organization?

What are the standard tools as recommended by the Shingo Institute?

These questions are posed by the Shingo Institute in their approach to systems-based thinking within organizations. The institute recommends the development of a system on a page. This is a document that gives an overview of the system – its owner, its aim, its workflows, reporting and schedules of activity along with a record of improvement activity that has taken place on the system itself to improve its effectiveness.

6.8. Aligning all systems to your story.

As mentioned earlier, the development of a genuine story and future vision of the organization is often a pivot point for a leadership team. Often it is the first time they have agreed their personal aspirations for the business in which they work and the team they support.

Regardless of what part of an organization or corporation you work in, as a leadership team you frame the culture of excellence within your team and align the aim and purpose of the systems in your local organization. By focusing on what is in your control, your story is real and can be lived by the vast majority of individuals in your organization. They will own their piece of the big picture.

> **The systems in your business must align and bring to life the genuine story, purpose and vison for your organization.**

Engagement is a contact sport. It is driven by the real compelling stories leaders tell of the type of organization they are trying to create – its purpose and responsibilities to employees, customers, and the planet. Our people interact with the story through the work that they do and the systems they interact with every day. This is the engagement engine of the business. Is the work aligned to the story? Do I get time and support to improve the work so it can better align to the story? Do I see my leaders as active players in the story?

The way in which we bring our story to life is through an aligned tiered management system.

6.9. Tier management systems: Learning from dancing bees

When a bee discovers a rich source of nectar, it returns to the hive and 'dances' to communicate the location of the bounty to other members of the hive. This dance has information on distance and direction of flight in relation to the sun. But one bee cannot reach out to the whole hive. Instead, the incoming bee's dance is watched and then accurately replicated by other bees throughout the hive. Within minutes the nectar harvesters are aligned on the location of this new source of bounty.

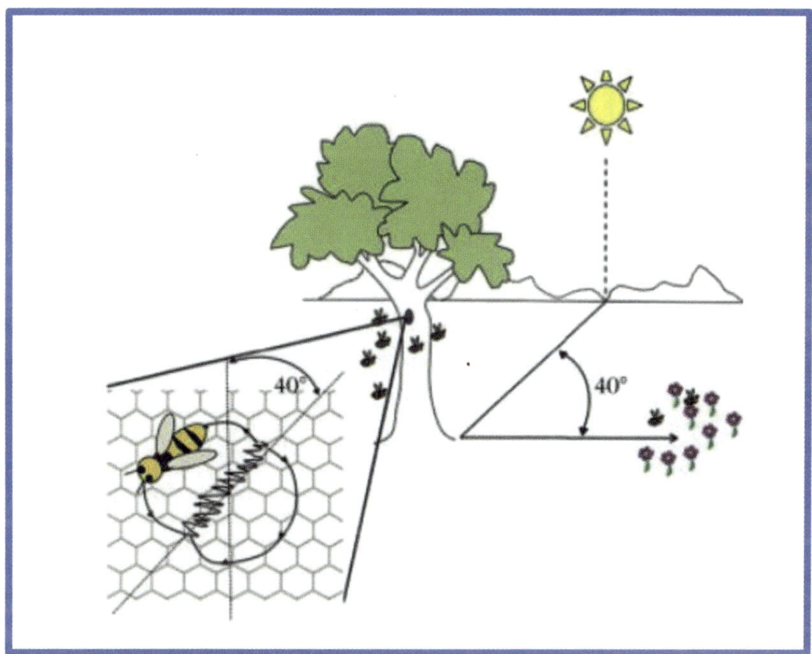

Figure 27: The honeybee dance. An example of tiered communication in nature? From Kaitlyn Preece and Madeleine Beekman, 'Honeybee waggle dance error: adaption or constraint? Unravelling the complex dance language of honeybees' (Preece & Beekman, 2014).

In organizations we look to communicate in two ways. First, we want to ensure the team know where they are going and why. Secondly, we want information for the teams to tell us how they are doing and what issues may need to be resolved or improved to help the team to their source of "pollen".

Most organizations rely on verbal communications, meetings, to convey information up down and across the organization. However, meetings are often seen as one of the greatest sources of waste in an organization. They are often the location where poor behaviors are expressed which negatively impact the performance and engagement of the individuals and teams attending them.

If you were to draw a map of all the meetings and connect the vital information flows between them what would that look like? Do the meetings have a real purpose or are they called to make one person's or one department's work easier? What are the necessary inputs and outputs of these meeting? How would we review the network of meetings to ensure they are delivering the necessary information at the right time to the right people?

In many organizations the meeting landscape has grown organically. There may have been an issue or miscommunication in the past and someone in their wisdom decided to set up a meeting to ensure it doesn't happen again. Sometimes organizations suffer from the tyranny of departments. Quality has their meeting structure. HSE their meetings. Both of which are separate to operations and planning and learning and development and... and... and... No wonder teams often complain about not having time to actually do work.

To start thinking differently about communication – up, down and across an organization – we need to think in terms of a system. We also need to start from the premise that we employ teams to add value by doing and supporting work. Meetings at their best are a necessary, non-value-added activity. At worst, they grow like an uncontrolled cancer to choke an organization driving poor behaviors in the process.

How many of your meetings are based around the control and management of problems in your organizations? Overdue CAPA, Budget overrun, Project timelines, shortage management. All creating a hidden factory consuming resources and time and leading to a great deal of frustration.

To start thinking about meeting structures differently we need to consider the aim of the system that supports them. Do we see it as part of our strategy deployment activity whereby we align groups in the same direction? Do we see it as part of our improvement system where we identify issues and resolve them as quickly as possible and continue to improve our performance? Or do we see it as part of our team engagement activity where we actively involve and communicate to team about the work that they do? In the end it is a mix of all of these. But if your organization is to think of meeting structures as a key system in your business, then you need to define the aim of that system and consider the five standard elements of the system which we mentioned above.

6.10. Building an effective tier management system

When reviewing structure or the tier management system, start by looking at the inbuilt cadence of your business. When does stuff have to happen? The daily / weekly / monthly / yearly cycles of what we must do. It is also worth reasserting who are the value-adding teams and who are the teams who support these teams in the work they do?

When we begin to reset meeting structures, we start to focus on the structure of tiers from the shopfloor value-adding teams up to senior management level. I am often struck by the level of detailed metrics at some senior teams' dashboard or score card. They are generally looking at metrics that are historic, often inaccurate, and with little bearing on managing or supporting the desired culture and behavior in the organization.

A well-designed tiered management system is the backbone of any organization. It should form the basis of all communication, process measurement, problem solving and improvement, and cultural development within the organization. It should also track the development of team skills and suggestions.

Tiered management can be a virtual or physical process which revolves around the activity within a given work group. The group may consist of an assembly line or part of it. A laboratory team, purchasing office or a design group. Each work group represents a unique part of the organization that must work synchronously with other parts of the business to ensure customer value is delivered as expected on time and in full and that business strategic objectives are met.

> It is the system that drives the practical implementation of business strategy as each department is aware and contributes to relevant critical success factors.
>
> It is the system that drives focused improvement based on the measurement of both leading and lagging measures. Where there is an issue with consistent performance, there should be a prioritised activity to improve that performance.
>
> The system should capture valuable ideas and suggestions to improve performance based on a targeted need. It should also recognise the individuals or teams who discovered the opportunity and implemented it.
>
> It is the system that enables and visualises accountability across the organization.
>
> It is the system that makes clear, at every level, what inputs and outputs to the process are necessary to achieve customer value.
>
> It is the system within which we can observe and develop leadership and coaching skills and where expressed behaviors can be seen and heard which will either be positive or negative with consequential impacts on business performance.
>
> It is the system within which the ideas and concerns of team members can be raised, listened to, reviewed and addressed.

The most important point to remember in revamping or implementing a tiered management process is that it is not about any individual board. It is about the conversations and quality of the culture that an individual board drives in each business unit. It is about how the information, culture, and performance that the board represents flows and impacts the next link in the chain of delivering value to your customers. It is a focus on the whole system not any one board, and how that system interacts with other critical systems.

6.11. Ownership and tiered management

There are many factory and office walls adorned with the skeletal remains of the last attempt at tier management. White boards with various coloured tape carefully arranged into boxes to contain this KPI or this project. To make a Tier board real for any work group it must be owned and developed by them. It must represent the inputs and outputs to their process and highlight the important areas that need to be managed carefully.

To march in with the standard template under one's arm is often a recipe for failure. It is better to build the board based on questions.

> Who are your customers in this department?
>
> What does good look like for these customers and how could we measure that?
>
> What are the inputs that this team knows are important in order for us to achieve what the customer needs?
>
> What are the things we could measure to ensure we highlight issues before impacting the customer?
>
> Do we understand what is important as a business focus over the coming years? The Critical Success factors (CSFs)? How does this department contribute to the CSFs?
>
> We understand the culture and behaviors the company needs; what would they look like in this department?
>
> Are there behaviors that are not helping and how could we manage them within the team?

What are the support teams you rely on and how often do you need to communicate with them in this area?

All these questions help the team to build a format that allows them to have structured and focused conversations around the work the team do every day or every week. The frequency of the meeting will very much depend on the cadence of the process. If we are in high volume multi lot manufacturing, we may need some form of check-in every hour. If we are in a back-office finance office a meeting every second day may be sufficient.

In all cases, the meeting structure, content and timing is clearly defined. Start time, duration, attendees, agenda, expected inputs and outputs are all documented to ensure that attendees' time at the meeting is respected and kept to a minimum. Where the team cannot deal with an issue themselves, it is formally escalated to the next level. The team should expect an update on that escalation that day or at the latest by their next meeting.

With time and maturity, tired meetings become the location where leaders can effectively observe the presence or absence of desired behaviors within the organization. How leaders interact with teams and create valuable engaging dialogue is a key skill by which they can either talk in or talk out the desired culture and behavior. An effective tiered management system provides the framework for powerful supportive and effective conversations. It is this system that allows leaders to step up to and back from issues by focusing on the quality of conversation and thinking within their team around the issue rather, than being pulled into the detail of the issue itself. This is an area we will review in the following chapter.

6.12. Tiered Management and Leader standard Work

The detailed make up and structure of a tiered management system is described in detail within the S A Partners Publication, *The Essence of Excellence*. In chapter five Hines and Butterworth describe the structure and cascade of tier management systems and the alignment of key performance indicators and key behavioural indicators throughout the system (Hines & Butterworth, 2019).

It is important to position the tiered management systems as the system that gives effect to the concept of servant leadership. Teams at the coal face are there to deliver value to customers every day. The role of leaders is to support and help these teams deliver that value by providing all the necessary skills, resources, and equipment at the right time and in the right condition to deliver this value. Leaders must also react supportively to escalated issues that are beyond the ability of the team themselves to resolve.

Tier management system is of no value unless it is supported by a formal process by which leadership engage with the system to ensure it is enabling the culture and behaviors to support these front-line teams.

Hines and Butterworth describe ten elements of a leader standard work system:

Meeting structure. What meetings are undertaken, by whom at what level of the organization and how information is passed from one level to another.

Meeting management. How these meetings are managed and what activity takes place.

Accountability management. Identifying who is accountable for what and how this is managed.

Meeting observation. Checking the meeting effectiveness and helping team leaders improve meetings.

Gemba walks. Making regular visits to the workplace for checking and coaching purposes.

Customer visits and benchmarking. Meeting with customers to understand their needs and translate them back to the organization and visiting other companies to compare activities, learn, and bring best practice back to the organization.

> **Reflection time.** Regularly spending time to reflect on what has happened so that new perspectives, knowledge and improvement can be achieved.
>
> **Recognition.** Giving praise and encouragement to create a sense of worth and engagement.
>
> **Performance management**. Planning, checking and acting upon the performance of employees.
>
> **Sharing.** Facilitating the transfer of knowledge from one area of the organization to another.
>
> (Hines & Butterworth, 2019)

In addition, Hines and Butterworth describe Leader standard work as the system that:

> Ensures that leaders develop the right culture by undertaking the right activity in the right style by:
>
> Understanding the roles and responsibilities of leaders at all levels
>
> Checking that activity is taking place to ensure business success
>
> Recognising people's contribution to success
>
> Identifying coaching and development opportunities so that:
>
> The whole organization engages its people, with the members taking initiative.
>
> (Hines & Butterworth, 2019).

Tier management without the backbone support of Leader standard work is just wallpaper. The meeting structure which a tier management system supports is about ensuring that the right conversation takes place at the right time in the right way.

How leaders effectively and positively interact with both Leader standard work and tier management systems will be covered in detail in the following chapter.

It is important to point out that within many organizations we have been asked to support, Leader standard work is viewed as a chore or a tick box exercise. Point seven in the list provided by Hines and Butterworth above is one important way to avoid this situation.

The system of Leader standard work must have an aim and a purpose as described for any system. It is critical that leadership teams give the space and time to reflect on information gathered by leaders and managers during their leader standard work activity. Having a common focus of observation during Go See activity can be a powerful way of uniting leadership teams to a common purpose. Going to the shopfloor with the agreed focus to assess, for example, whether teams understand the vision and critical success factors, or checking that problem-solving is happening effectively across the organization. Do we observe the presence of agreed values such as respect and customer focus? These are all questions that can be reflected upon and discussed within the leadership community. This reflective process of seeing the reality holds up a mirror to leadership teams, asking:

> Are we leading the way we intended to lead to achieve our purpose?
>
> Are we supporting the culture and behavior we agreed was critical for our success as a business?

Powerful questions to ensure the leadership remain focused on their responsibility to manage and support the appropriate culture and behaviors in their organization.

6.13. Work Systems Understanding the work and the ways we need to work, together

'Most of what we call 'management' consists of making it difficult for people to get their work done.'

-Dr. Peter Drucker

Now more than ever leaders and managers must take greater interest in and focus on the work undertaken by their teams. Regardless of any disconnected thinking or inefficiencies at higher levels of the organization, as a leader or manager I can influence my team's approach to the work that they do every day.

As a junior engineer one of my first go-to sources of reference on work design was the International Labour Office (ILO) *Introduction to Work Study* (Kanawaty, 1992). It is disappointing to see that this focus on the science of how work works has been lost in many organizations or passed on to the shoulders of an already overstretched continuous improvement team.

As the pending crisis of our overuse and exploitation of the resources of our life support system, planet earth, is now a reality, our focus as leaders must be to design and manage work in a way that ensures the most effective and efficient use of resources.

> The management of an enterprise is responsible for seeing that the enterprise resources (land and buildings, materials, energy, machines and equipment, human resources) are combined in the best possible way to achieve the highest productivity
>
> (Kanawaty, 1992)

The ILO used the following well know diagram to explain the role of management.

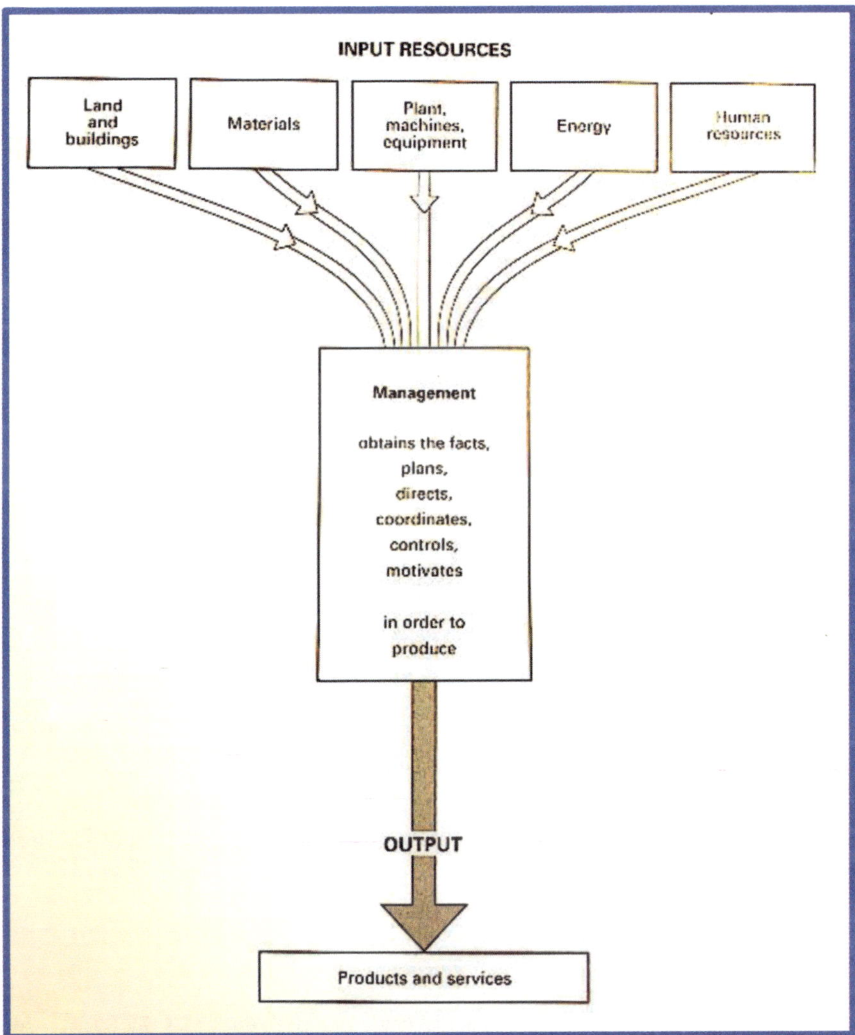

Figure 28: Original International labor office illustration of the responsibilities of management (Kanawaty, 1992).

Given our current environmental challenges I suggest the model should be updated as follows.

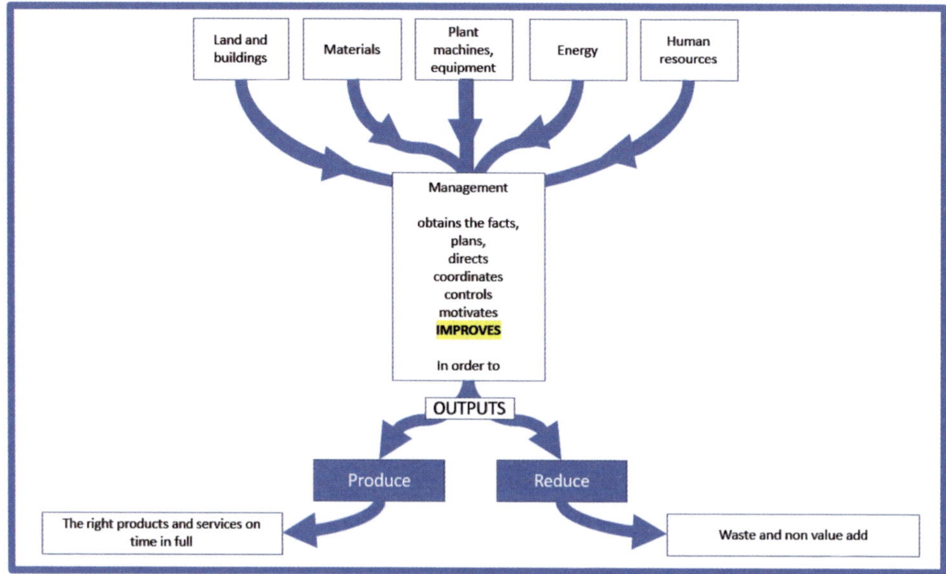

Figure 29: The author's addition to the original illustration.

Many leaders can see an illustration like this and think of the automobile assembly line or metal cutting and milling operations. But as we understand the impact of our energy hungry data sector and the inherent inefficiencies within our back-office processes, which often drive larger inefficiencies across supply chains, the delays and overburden in our health systems, the study and understanding of the nature of the work is equally applicable in these environments.

To engage a team with the work that they do there are a few basic points to consider:

What is the true nature of the work that most of the value-adding members of your team do?

What are the behaviors that govern the way the team constructively work together to ensure success?

Are we measuring success the right way?

Do we understand and visualize the full impact of sub-optimal levels of performance on colleagues, customers, and planet?

As we mentioned earlier in this book, transformative participation is only achievable where individuals truly believe the story behind the purpose and intent of an organization. Platitudes and aspirations of greatness and improved shareholder values seldom win the hearts and minds of the people we truly need to engage. The attitude to work and work systems must be aligned to the purpose and culture of the organization.

We see two manifestations of this.

Scenario 1:

The actual work that I do may be boring and mundane, but I am learning new skills, giving me better understanding of the work and how to manage and improve the work. I am also engaged with the way my company truly supports local communities. I see my leaders actively participating in the process. During these events there are no chevrons. We all have the same passion in what we are doing. The more successful we are as a business the more of the good work we can do, and I understand that.

Scenario 2:

The work that I do is complex; we are constantly firefighting – this is exciting for me. I was learning new stuff, but we now see the same issues again and again. Our work systems force us to approach things like investigations a certain way, often not giving the time we need. We have a corporate social responsibility programme which is part of my annual performance expectations. I try to get involved when I can. I seldom see leaders at these events and if they do show they are not really present.

Which example is closer to a sense of deep excellence?

6.14. So, what is the work?

Having someone sit down in front of you and ask you straight out *'so how do your team add value?'* can be a perplexing question. Often, we fall into *'we just do stuff'* mindset, without really thinking how the *'do stuff'* aligns with other departments *'do stuff'* to ultimately deliver value!

A subdepartment of a finance organization in a large multinational explained their value add as writing financial reports! The conversation became interesting when clarity was sought on what the reports were for and how they helped the business. What made a good report compared to a bad report? Are the reports issued at the correct cadence to match the speed of decision making in the business? How have the reports been improved to improve the overall performance of the business?

The team had not clearly defined how their reports add value by providing accurate data at the right time to allow the business to maintain or change focus or to ensure it continued to provide value to customers and stakeholders.

It may be time to take a step back and ask yourself the following questions,

> What is the specific way your organization adds value? (Forget about Shareholders for the moment. If you do right for your customers, your Shareholders will be OK!)
>
> How does your team's activity align with the 'purpose and story' of the business?
>
> How well can you articulate that story and that alignment?
>
> How do your team add value in a way that contributes to the overall success of the business?
>
> What are the key elements that must be in place to constantly deliver that value?

Do your measures reflect the management of these key elements to enable success (leading measures), or do your measures reflect things that we can no longer influence (lagging measures)?

How are those key elements monitored, managed and improved?

What are the key skills needed in the team to deliver the work?

What are the behaviors that help your team win more often?

What is the quality and usability of the work, standards and processes that describe the work?

If, as a leader, you have not considered the above questions, it will be almost impossible to develop a sustainable culture of deep excellence within your team.

6.15. Winning or losing behaviors within the work system?

Go and observe deeply the way in which people interact with their peers and colleagues in their own and other departments. The way in which they make decisions, the way they conduct continuous improvement and solve problems. Is it once off or intermittent improvement or is there a relentless drive to improve the quality of work and value to the customer?

There are clues to the undercurrents of culture if we look for the themes and patterns that present themselves. It takes practice to see these, and it is even more difficult when you, as a leader, are part of the infrastructure and culture behind them. However, it is an important exercise to undertake. Are the behaviors observed within front line teams a reflection of the shadow cast by leaders?

So, what are the winning behaviors we might observe in your organization?

How about the way in which an engineer, instead of pushing operators aside as she investigates a problem with a piece of machinery, listens intently to the experience of the operators. She might work with the operators to watch and trial ways to understand the root cause of the issue. Once potential root causes are identified they are presented back to a wider group of operators for their inputs. With the inputs taken on board and maybe more confirmatory trials taken place, *the operators and the engineer* come up with effective countermeasures that are standardized and captured with revised procedures or work instructions.

How about the way in which a salesperson might spend time with a customer to really understand their needs? Going out of their way to support the customer in solving their problem and through solving that problem identify new business opportunities to be shared with the wider sales team.

How about the way a supervisor encourages their team to bring forward ways in which the process that they do every day can be improved? Who then actively reviews each potential improvement with their team and gives the team the time and support to implement their improvement ideas?

Within our organizations there are day-to-day, week to week expressions of behaviors that enable teams to win more often. There are also behaviors that create obstacles and frustrations in the way work takes place.

As we explained in the previous chapter, as leaders we must be sensitive to and observe and reward these winning behaviors. Equally, leaders must have the sensitivity, persistence, and skill to challenge and effectively correct where these behaviors are absent.

6.16. The Right Measures within the work system.

Look at the key performance indicators in your department or organization. If we first trust that when green is green then outcomes will be good and the measure is now red, we should ask: what are the things that would have prevented the red?

Take a simple example. The team has not met sales target for the quarter. Sales arise from a funnel of contacts, leads, proposals and eventually winning work. The seeds for a successful sales quarter are generally set in the previous two quarters. So, how much do we as team focus on the quality of contact and leads? Or the quality of the initial and follow-up meetings with potential customers. What about the promptness with which we respond to requests for a proposal and the follow up once a proposal is issued. All of these are the leading activities that give rise to the lagging measure of quarterly sales performance.

Consider then the behaviors that support these leading measures. Maybe speed and responsiveness to customer enquiry and follow up. It could be the contact curiosity and interest in the customer and what enables their success. It could be good personal time management which allows dedicated time for dedicated tasks. Some of these behaviors could be measured such as the response time to customer query. But it cannot only be the response time. We also need to have mechanisms to review the quality of the response either through customer feedback or direct observations.

6.17. *Pulling it all together*

Delivering for the business involves the constant interplay between the identification, standardization and continual improvement of critical work methods and the systems that support them. These systems must be design and managed purposefully to enable the behaviors and culture necessary to ensure ongoing and sustainable improvement of the businesses performance.

Systems provide the architecture by which leaders can either talk and coach improvement into a business or talk it out. The systems provide the check and balancing point to ensure teams stay away from the ancient parts of their brain. Remaining instead in the higher, more creative, problem-solving areas where improvement and innovation flourish.

As we will see in the next chapter the ability of leaders to hold high quality conversations in a way that is supportive to the team and their endeavors is a vital leadership skill in managing and interacting with these critical business systems effectively.

7 The new language of leadership

7.1. Influencing and developing the team - Leadership for deep excellence

How do you as a leader want to lead your team? How do you want the people who work in your organization to feel on their way into work? What will excite you as you meet people and listen to them talk about their work and their challenges around the work? These are all questions to consider in relation to how you as the senior leader with the support of your peers on the senior leadership want to define the culture of your organization. The environment where 'they leave their brains at the factory gate as they clock in for work' is a dated but still very applicable description of the culture we don't want.

As the leader, whatever it is you want to achieve in your business – spoiler alert – you cannot do it on your own. You can only work through the team. It's funny but, in early conversations with leaders, you can tell a lot from how they talk about the business. Sentences that begin with 'I want to...' or 'The future will be...' don't bode well. Expressions such as 'People are just not holding themselves to account' or 'They're not engaged in the big picture...' only add to concerns around the quality of the conversation and the commitment of leadership to real transformational change. Conversations that begin with, 'Here, it is all about the people...' or 'Our focus is about making a positive impact in what we do... ', are potential indications of a more enlightened conversation.

Your team members are all individuals. The challenges you face and resources you have available vary. Resources in the form of raw materials, energy etc. are fast becoming more costly and scarce. You, as the senior leader, and your leadership team cannot solve these issues. But you can focus on creating and supporting the appropriate cultural environment in the business where your teams understand, manage and eventually resolve these issues for you.

New expectations of employees have been developing and have been accelerated by the COVID pandemic. Expectations around wellbeing, higher purpose and personal growth are part of the growing expectations of workforces around the world.

Mercer, in their *Global Talent Trends Study 2022: The Rise of the Relatable Organization*, outline five key areas of focus in developing and retaining talent as a strategy to navigate the predicted uncertainty of the coming decades. The report, which summarizes responses from eleven thousand respondents is highly informative on the future structures and expectations of how work works (Mercer, 2022). The five key areas are:

> **Reset for relevance.**
>
> *Build resilience by leading with values and an adaptive design.*
>
> The events of the past two years have left an indelible mark on investor, employee and consumer attitudes. The new world of work — more nuanced and personalized — demands a reset of priorities. It requires new skills around listening, learning and adapting to identify and address unmet needs.
>
> **Work in partnership.**
>
> *Create equitable, transparent, and rewarding relationships.*
>
> People no longer want to work for a company; they want to work with a company. The future of work depends on flatter and more networked talent models, fueled by a more flexible, fungible and, for many, a more globally dispersed workforce. This represents a shift in the social contract of work, one that will succeed only if everyone feels they are getting a fair deal.
>
> **Deliver on total well-being**
>
> *Nurture a healthy workforce with benefits that matter.*
>
> The pandemic exposed and worsened the health and wealth gaps for different populations, underscoring that accessibility and

affordability of care is not enough. The well-being ROI that matters today is less about a return on investment (focused on reducing health-related costs) and more about what makes a difference to safeguard the current and future welfare of the workforce.

Build for employability

Meet future work needs with a skills-based organization.

The significant supply and demand gap in both skills and workers has highlighted the role that organizations play not just in ensuring their own sustainability but also in safeguarding the future employability of their people.

Harness collective energy

Unlock potential with human-centered work environments

The "future of work" was already challenging enterprises before COVID-19, but it was seen as a long-term play. The pandemic accelerated the timeline and exponentially increased the urgency to adopt new business models, new ways of working and new technologies. Ideas that were once met with skepticism and reluctance are now solutions to some of the biggest challenges of our time — and while people are exhausted, they are also more optimistic that these changes will ultimately drive a more balanced future of work.

(Mercer, 2022)

Leaders within organizations need to be aware and possess the necessary skills to address these engagement areas while clearly defining the organizational culture, behavior and systems that support them.

7.2. The untapped power of conversation:

> 'I cannot doubt that language owes its origin to the imitation and modification, aided by signs and gestures, of various natural sounds, the voices of other animals, and man's own instinctive cries.'
>
> -Charles Darwin, 1871

Remembering back to the evolutionary legacy covered in chapter one, it is easy to forget the relatively insignificant amount of time we have spent as sentient beings on this planet. It is even more unnerving when you consider the development of organized societal structures and the development of complex language.

Various researchers estimate the development of language in our species between fifty to one hundred and fifty thousand years ago (Barham & Everett, 2021).

Language has been the cornerstone of our social and societal development. Yet our need to communicate effectively – to share ideas, intentions and beliefs, or to focus and align activity – gives rise to the same challenges today as our ancestors faced many years ago. In business today, leaders often lack the skills to use the power of language effectively – to employ conversation to engage their teams in the goals and objectives and the 'Why' of the business.

As a race we communicate with each other through our talk. Our effective use of language in the way we communicate has a direct impact on the mindset and ultimately the behavior of those we communicate to.

Think of your own situation. Can you remember a situation where the way someone spoke to you either inspired you or left you deflated? Have you been surprised by the way your innocent conversation was interpreted by others? Or the way an apparently clear set of instructions were completely misconstrued?

The quality of the talk has a direct impact on an individual's state of mind and ultimately the behaviors and actions we observe arising from our conversations.

7.3. The quality of talk

Through numerous interactions within leadership teams, and watching leader and team member engagements, we often observe and hear the wrong types of conversations. These conversations are misaligned with the actual intent of the conversation. Both parties leave with very different understanding from the conversation. When this becomes dominant in the way key leaders communicate it creates very real issues around conformance, accountability recognition, trust and ultimately business performance.

Miscommunication is surprisingly easy to spot as an outsider to the business. You recognize the symptoms; the leader is in dialogue with a team member and the reaction from the team member is one of confusion, disbelief / frustration, or simply a blank expression. There are obviously things left unsaid. Questions that should have been asked and were not. Clarification given or sought is absent. The style of dialogue and the reception of that dialogue is not aligned to the requirements or needs of the deliverer or the recipient. As a result, team members regularly and consistently underperform despite saying they understand what is required.

But why is this so easy to observe as an outsider and yet it goes unseen or unaddressed within the organization? Based on our interview and coaching activity we see several reasons for this.

The leader is just not aware or sensitive enough to the situation. They have communicated and done what they had to do, it's up to the team to get on with it!

The dominant environment is not 'safe enough' to support constructive challenge or seeking clarification.

The leader knows there are things left unsaid but lacks the confidence and skill to ask the right questions effectively. They may have challenged in the past, but people ended up getting upset! It is easier not to ask the difficult questions!

An environment has developed where formal meeting activity has become a compliance-based tick box activity. Real work and issues are addressed outside of the meeting and rely on personal relationship networks within the business.

The best place to observe the quality of conversation in an organization is to look for the structured formal setting where a particular type of conversation is expected to take place. We reference a case study below where teams were engaged in dialogue at their department tier board.

We believe the tiered management system, as discussed earlier, is one of the most important systems within any business. It should align team focus, based on strategy and priorities. It should indicate performance and facilitate problem solving and continuous improvement. At these meetings we should observe effective cross-functional conversations and the identification of opportunities for recognition and skill development. Other formal examples may include structured problem solving or Kaizen activity, team meetings, or one to one reviews. All these situations provide opportunities for skillful purposeful dialogue. That is the right conversation in the right place at the right time.

The quality and impact of a conversation on the receiver's state of mind and resulting behavior is dependent on the way in which the conversation is delivered. Normally, when we experience the kind of conversations we are expecting, we are content with the interaction. Whether this is the right outcome is another matter!

In a social setting, vagueness in outcomes resulting from a conversation can be tolerated to some degree. In a formal business environment, we need to have a higher level of expectation that the conversation we hold to direct, engage, or provide support to our teams results in the outcomes expected rather than creating more problems and issues to be managed.

7.4. Better Dialogue = Better Behaviors = Better Results

The curious thing about our use of language is that all too often we forget that there are three elements to the process of conversation.

> The quality transmission of the message (my talk).
>
> The receipt of the message (the individual's ability and readiness to receive the message).
>
> The understanding and translation of the message (was the message understood as intended).

If any of these elements of the conversation are missing the result is suboptimal or at worst the opposite to what was intended.

Patterns of dialogue are often learned from those around us – it's not unusual for a team to start to take on the conversational traits of their boss – either because they see this as the way that someone else gets things done or because it is the only way we have ever seen things done. We may adapt our natural preferences because it feels like there is only ever one style of conversation that gets through to others. It may be the conversations that get us the attention of our boss, as they see and hear their influence on our form of conversation. It may also be because it's only this style of voice that the receiver seems to respond to (even though it may not be our natural tendency) – left unmanaged, this means we can develop very specific and often unhelpful language patterns.

The quality of my talk will depend on the skillful way I read the situation and move between a conversation style that appropriately balances the main dialogue types (or voices) of telling, suggesting, or asking. Indeed, depending on the high skill and motivation of the individual, the situation may demand that we are present and just listen.

The balance is set by the competency and confidence of the giver and receiver of the dialogue. Telling a highly experienced self-motivated individual what they should do in each situation is a sure way to switch them off. Equally, coaching a beginner by asking them how they think they should approach a given situation can result in high stress or over confidence, neither of which are good for long term outcomes.

Compartmentalizing the 'voices' used into the dialogue types of Ask (explore), Suggest (position) and Tell (direct) can help a leader pause and consider carefully the message they may be hearing or delivering. Within each of these three types of dialogue, there are further variations in how we can Ask, Suggest or Tell, enabling our Asking to be more open, more focused or more analytical, our Suggesting to be more personal, more neutral or more provisional, and our Telling to be more directing, improving or deciding. We have a repertoire of nine potential voices: inquire, probe, diagnose, advocate, articulate, advise, direct, challenge and evaluate. All of which create signposts for our conversation and help us to achieve purposeful quality conversations that are focused on the task at hand.

We all have preferential or simply habitual styles of dialogue. A lack of awareness of these dominant tendencies in the way leaders interact with their teams can lead to miscommunication, breakdowns in relationships and trust, and an inability of the team member to perform as expected.

When we are expecting to be asked our opinion on something, and what actually happens is someone tells us what to do, this often invokes a feeling of anger or frustration – especially if done repeatedly.

When we are expecting to be told or directed to do something but then are actually asked, especially if this is an out of character style of communication, we can become suspicious of the interaction.

There is a halfway point where suggestions are offered to us (when we are expecting either to be told or to be asked) where we have a feeling of neutrality or indifference. Over time repeated use of this misaligned conversation provokes either a frustration or a "switching off" effect.

These three main forms of dialogue form a broad framework for us to start to be deliberate in selecting the appropriate dialogue in each circumstance. There are a number of self-perception tools available to help leaders understand their own dominant voices. VoicePrint is one of the tools S A Partners team has used extensively in our activities over the last fifteen years.

7.5. Understanding My Talk

Self-Perception tools such as VoicePrint help individuals understand their preferential tendencies in relation to their use of language. They help individuals understand the patterns of talk allowing them over time to learn how to modify their dominant voices to ensure the right dialogue is used at the right time.

Self-perception analysis alongside 360 feedback help leaders develop their skill and sensitivity in their use of language by exposing their current tendencies in their use of language. With practice, leaders purposefully develop a more rounded, balanced, set of language skills. This awareness and skill allows leaders to target their use of language to purposefully influence the mindset, behaviors and resulting outcomes of individual and team discussions.

Being more aware of the impact of the quality of dialogue allows leaders to consider what is the desired outcome of both formal and informal conversations with peers and team members. When adopted across a group of leaders and managers, a common focus on improving the quality of conversations can have a significant difference in how they communicate, solve problems and get better results more often.

EXPLORING (Ask)	Inquire	To ask open-mindedly in order to find out more. The voice that seeks to understand others.
	Probe	To dig deeper, going beyond or behind what is already apparent. The voice that calls for further detail or disclosure.
	Diagnose	To analyse in order to come to an understanding. The voice that seeks to connect and make sense of information.
POSITIONING (Suggest)	Advocate	To hold a personal position or view, either for or against. The voice that pushes a case or argues for a viewpoint.
	Advise	To suggest a course of action or a way of thinking. The voice that offers a proposal or solution.
	Articulate	To describe and clarify in a precise, neutral, matter-of-fact way. The voice that combines and summarises other inputs
CONTROLLING (Tell)	Direct	To call (or recall) attention to a responsibility, required standard or boundary. The voice of authority that demands compliance.
	Challenge	To interrupt in order to improve the quality of what is happening. The voice that re-focuses.
	Evaluate	To weigh up thoroughly and objectively, considering both strengths and weaknesses. The voice that deliberates and assesses.

Figure 30: The VoicePrint Model © Talk Wise Ltd All Rights Reserved.

Part of the process of developing skills in the use of language is an activity where leaders spend time listening to their own use of language in a coaching environment. We meet many leaders who claim to have good coaching experience however, during training programmes, we ask permission to listen in and record their conversations with their direct reports. The situation may be a one-to-one development review or an update on progress on a project or goal. While the initial flow of conversation may be stilted it is amazing how quickly the leader and their report fall into their normal conversational styles.

When the conversation is played back, leaders are often shocked to hear the poor quality of their conversation. As the training activity progresses and teams become accustomed to the methodology the participant in the conversation is asked to listen to simple things such as:

> How much time did you spend speaking compared to the coachee?
>
> What was the balance of conversation between telling, suggesting and asking?
>
> Were their questions open or closed? Did you make your points clear?
>
> Did you clarify the individual's understanding with an open question that helps you know they actually understood?
>
> Did you listen to the response, or did you launch into your next question?

These sessions are very enlightening for the leader whose dominant voices can often be clearly heard. The beauty of understanding the power of the effective use of language is that it is a skill that individuals can learn despite an underlying personality trait. With practice the quality of conversation can be significantly improved. At its simplest, changing the way a question is phrased can help us achieve better outcomes.

Imagine a situation where we have our own thoughts as to why an individual behaved a certain way. How we ask the question allows us as leaders to get to the real crux of what's going on.

> When we ask – **why** did you make that decision – we are likely to get a conscious stream of justifications

If we were to ask **how** you came to those conclusions, we might get closer to understanding the thought process, and the underlying perceptions – giving us further opportunities to explore and develop reasoning and understanding around the issue.

7.6. Our default use of language

It is also important to understand that our default tendency in our use of language is not ideal. A widespread tendency is to avoid the correcting and challenging voices. Based on review of over two thousand self-perception assessments carried out using the VoicePrint self-perception tool there is a common tendency for leaders and managers to avoid these difficult conversations. Is it any wonder that leaderships often complain of a lack of accountability or adherence to standards in their organization?

Through the development of language skills around inquiring and probing voices, leaders can direct in an informed way which involves and respects people, creating an opportunity for learning, better understanding, and aligning around what is important.

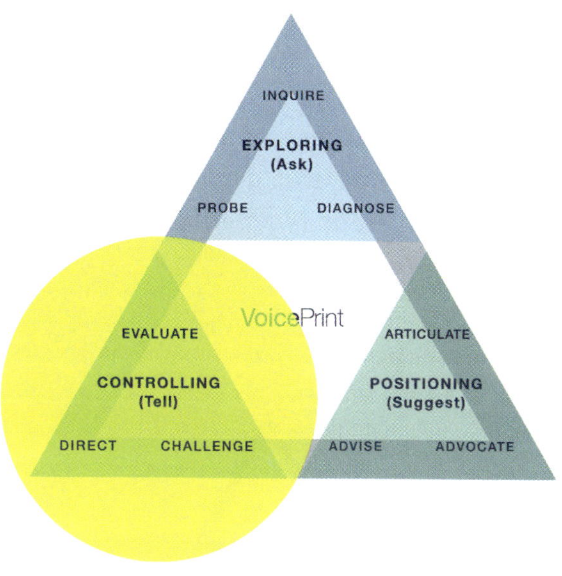

Figure 31: The VoicePrint Controlling voices. Directing, Challenging and Evaluating voices tend to be the weaker voices with leadership and management groups. © Talk Wise Ltd All Rights Reserved.

Leaders who claim to direct effectively can tend to be overzealous especially in their correction, leaving the individual on the receiving end with feelings of being singled out, personally attacked and punished. In a similar vein, excessive inquiry can lead to a feeling of interrogation on the part the receiver.

The consequences of weak voices on the other hand can be equally unhelpful. Weak use of probe and diagnose voices, may leave team members feeling the conversation is superficial or that you are not really concerned about the issue at hand.

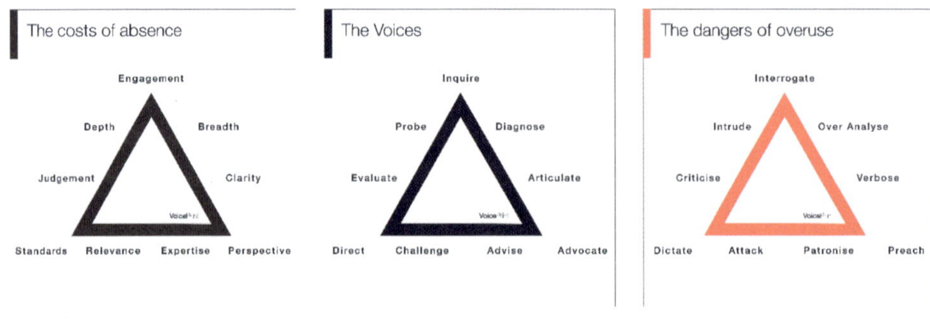

Figure 32: The VoicePrint model representing the balance of voices. © Talk Wise Ltd All Rights Reserved

There can be many different reasons why an individual makes relatively little use of a particular voice. The only sound generalization is to consider how the quality and impact of a conversation is affected when a particular voice is missing. The absence of inquiry costs engagement. The absence of direction costs standards. The absence of advocacy costs perspective. And so on.

Our practical experience in supporting this focus on dialogue proves to the authors that awareness and skillful use of language can result in profound sustainable improvement in a team's and thereby organization's performance. The quality of language used in effect results in leaders either talking in or talking out a sustainable culture of improvement within an organization.

Skillful use of dialogue is a critical underlying skill to ensure the effectiveness of key signature systems such as the leadership system, including leader standard work and tier management which is the system by which improvement happens and is supported within organizations. These signature systems all provide the opportunity for purposeful deliberate conversation styles that will have a direct impact on the behaviors and thereby the actions of individuals across the organization.

7.7. Structuring more deliberate conversations

'If you do not know how to ask the right question, you discover nothing.'

-W. Edwards Deming

Effective leadership is based on the effective use of dialogue and, the ability to flex between the four key leadership roles of instructor, mentor, coach and delegator.

The adoption of the role and the style of conversation associated with that role is a key skill of good leadership. It is also dependent on the leader's acute awareness of the competency, confidence, and mindset of the individual or team on the opposite side of the conversation.

Good leadership conversations are based on the quality of the questions we ask and our understanding of the mindset of the individual or team. A good leader is constantly searching for the underlying behaviors necessary for the team or individual to achieve their goal. It is therefore as much about the times we don't speak as it is about the times we do!

Figure 33: Leadership craft for Sustainable Excellence. © S A Partners.

The leadership for excellence model focuses on four key areas.

1. The goal or objective of the individual or team.
2. How I match my role in the conversation as either Instructor, Mentor, Coach or Delegator to the needs of the team member or the situation.
3. How I carefully match the language to effectively influence the mindset of the individual and their resulting behaviors.
4. Defining the form collaboration will take, given the fact that there are structured formal situations such as tier meetings, problem solving activity, one to one review, where quality of the dialogue and expectation can be defined. But there are also informal settings, an office drop-in to discuss an issue, conversations in the canteen, where we still need to

ensure the quality of the dialogue is at a level capable of positively affecting the actions and behaviors of the individual following that conversation.

Any individual may find themselves in any of the quadrants depending on what they are working on at any time. Just because someone is an expert in their field does not mean they are an expert in all the tasks or objectives that have been set. Therefore, understanding of the competence, confidence, or motivation for the task up front is critical to ensure the right dialogue is achieved.

7.8. The Objective

Much has been written about the importance of setting clear goals, so no need to repeat that here. But good supportive leadership conversations begin with clarity of the objective. Is it specific, measurable, achievable, realistic and time bound. The acronym SMART is commonly used to define an objective setting but, just as a poorly defined problem statement can hinder our ability to focus on resolving a problem effectively, a poorly defined objective is equally wasteful. Looking for SMART objectives, as first expressed by George T. Doran, allows us to ask questions about the objectives of an individual or team. REF

Having good conversations around the structure and targets of the objective allow you, as a leader, to listen to the quality of thought and conversation from the individual or team relating to the objective. SMART objectives also put a responsibility on the leader to ensure that the objective is in fact attainable given a realistic assessment of current constraints and challenges.

No doubt it is possible to create very detailed project plans and a charter on building an ice bridge to the sun or creating ten new revenue generating product launches within the year. However, both may be equally unrealistic given the circumstances of the team and business at that time!

7.9. HEAD HEART HANDS

In all cases when reviewing the task and conversation we are about to have with the individual or team we need to first examine the head heart and hands status of the individual or team. That is the competence the confidence and the motivation of the individual.

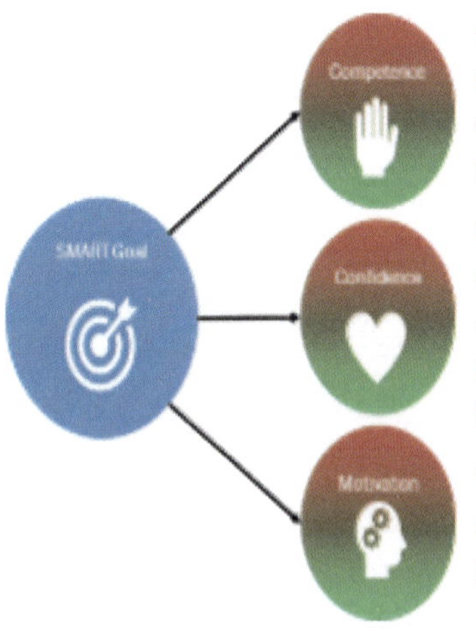

What is the level of competence of the individual or team given the task at hand. Is this completely new stretch zone territory or familiar.

What level of confidence is there around the task and achieving the desired result. Over confidence may signal lack of understanding. Lack of confidence may lead to fear and hesitancy and overcomplexity.

What sense of motivation is there around the activity to people want to do this and why is it important to them?

Figure 34: The Head, Heart and Hands. © S A Partners

Conversation around the head heart and hands can lead to better understanding and commitment to the task at hand from the team and help the leader fulfill an effective leadership role in supporting the individual or team.

7.10. The leadership sustainable excellence model in detail:

In the instructor quadrant of the model, we see the recipient as a beginner.

Typically, in this situation, the recipient in the conversation lacks either specific knowledge or competence to complete a task, with sometimes the motivation to do it. Very often new beginners are actually very excited about the challenge that a new task brings (excitable puppy syndrome), but we shouldn't as leaders read this as knowing what it is that needs to be done!

The role of a leader in this type of situation is one of **Instructor**; they help to create clarity on the standards required, challenging previous assumptions or thoughts, and giving good critique on what is or has been going well and what needs to be improved. Clarity is at its highest in this situation and communication should leave very little room for ambiguity for the learner's next steps. Most often the leader will make decisions about what needs to be done.

Whilst we say that most of the dialogue is using **Tell or Directing** type voices, this doesn't mean that questions are not asked, but too many of these at the developmental stage of a learner will leave the individual feeling vulnerable and rudderless.

The creation of clarity is key here – how many times have we been in a situation where a leader has given instructions, and left the team or individual with a closed question "is that clear"? "Do you understand?".

From a behavioral perspective when we are learning, it is often quite difficult to ask for further clarity on a situation – you don't know what you don't know; our motivation is often high even thought our ability is not and we will go away and give it a go, not knowing what areas of unknowns lie ahead. In this situation, much better questions to ask after having given instruction are about how that clarity has landed:

> 'So, tell me the main elements you understand about what you need to do next?'
>
> 'What are the key areas you think you need to watch out for?'

As a leader we will then understand what is and what is not understood. These early points of clarity help keep our learners focused and likely to be able to achieve the short- and long-term goals of the tasks more effectively.

Inevitably as the beginner progresses into a learner, the dialogue style of the leader needs to adjust too. Perhaps the learner motivation has dipped a little as the realization of their true competence level is understood, perhaps they are struggling with how to handle new situations or are coming across hurdles that are familiar, but they have never mastered how to overcome.

In the **Mentoring** mode, the conversation should be much more open than in the beginner mode, we should hear the learner ask more questions and be open to sharing the experiences and issues they are having; pulling a little more on the leader for their perspective and advice to help them make some decisions about their next steps. At this point, reinforcement of the good progress that is being made and perhaps even some awareness raising of what is not being done as against the leader expectations. These conversations are used to help the learner grow in confidence and to acknowledge their shortcomings and implications of any issues that are arising in the work they are undertaking.

The head, heart and hands aspect are arguably the most critical to identify in the learner quadrant. The need for the leader to listen carefully and adjust their dialogue appropriately is paramount.

A learner can be keen to progress, humble, accepting, and open to what is not working but can equally seem defeated or dispassionate about what needs to be done. The leader's sensitivity to what the problems are, where they are seated and how to handle them are key to keeping the learner progressing.

If leaders stick in this learner zone with an individual or team for too long or continue to give beginner-like instructions – the recipients of the conversations will quickly become frustrated – the dialogue here should be inclusive, and the transfer of ownership should be moving from manager to learner. We make collaborative decisions and explore things together.

The role of the leader here is very much to start to move towards a more curious stance and take away their own assumptions and views of the world... working towards a collective understanding of possibilities. Taking the responsibility for personal development of skills, clarity of direction and confidence should be at the heart of these conversations.

7.11. Coach and Delegator roles:

Work by Mihaly Csikszentmihalyi reveals that tasks that challenge and stretch us but not excessively so, and from which our efforts gain positive feedback, give us pleasure, and develop our sense of confidence and self-worth. Identifying and monitoring an individual's or team's 'Stretch Zone' is a key leadership skill in developing true engagement and learning within the organization.

Csikszentmihalyi, M, 2008, *Flow*: *The Psychology of Optimal Experience*

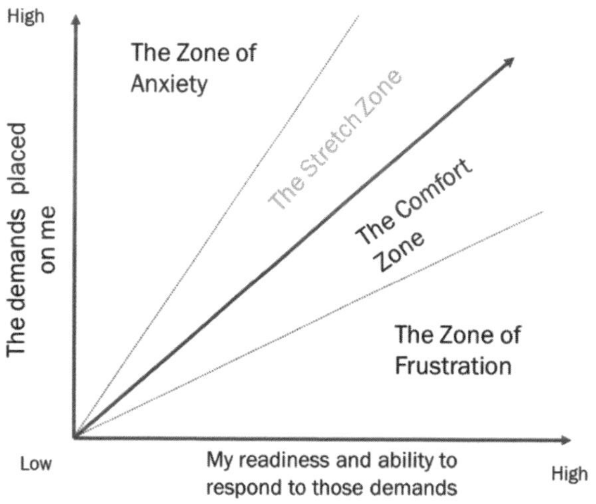

Figure 35: The stretch one of learning

It important to be aware that even expert individuals can become beginners again given a new situation or challenge. Understanding the situation of the individual or team allows us to get clarity on my role as leader.

Must I provide clear **instruction** as the situation is new and there is a clear lack of know-how, confidence, confidence, or motivation? Here instructions need to be clear and often must be repeated back to ensure clarity of understanding. Specific standards and procedures will need to be referenced and specific stakeholders identified.

Is my role to be one of a **mentor** providing guidance and experience as needed as the situation shows evidence of experience, self-motivation, competence, or confidence. Or do I need to act as a coach where in many ways I act as a sounding board for the development and formation of concepts and ideas which arise from within the individuals themselves?

Or am I in the enviable situation where all my careful development activity has paid off and I now have a highly competent individual or team in front of me to which I am confident in the **delegation** of decisions and activity? The interaction here is more a discussion on the decision taken and their outcomes.

By developing a greater focus on the quality of language used by the leader and the form of the collaborative relationship between the leader and their reports, the quality of conversation greatly improves. As a result, the mindset and confidence of individuals and teams increases, to support observable behaviors that are aligned to the desired culture of the organization.

7.12. Is coaching always the answer?

The way in which we ask questions can be crucial to the creation of a learning, growing and improving organization. An organization where managers ask questions, rather than provide solutions, develops teams rather than judging them and bemoaning their shortfalls.

Coaching demands that we listen closely to the conversation at hand and to let our minds go from our opinions and judgements to a state where we can ask deep and thoughtful questions of the coachee. If done well the process builds confidence with the individual and allows them to find the answers they need from within themselves. It is this ability to ask thoughtful questions which is a key coaching skill.

Often, we meet managers who insist they coach. But the reality of what we hear and feed back in recorded conversations is repeated suggestive questions indicating the way the individual should move forward.

Suggestion creates a not-so-subtle form of dependency.

Leaders get caught by the **"Curse of Suggestion".** An example is where a team member tells you, the leader, about an idea or has a solution (X) in mind for a problem they are facing. As a leader you listen but are faced with the irresistible urge to build upon the idea edging towards the (2X) outcome.

> "Ah yes that's great I hear you and understand, but have you thought about doing A, B or C as well" or "could we do it this way instead?"

This pattern of leader to team member conversation over time creates a level of dependency, stifling of the team member's opportunity to learn from experience. In turn leaders are drawn into problems that should be solved by the team. Team members learn the pattern quickly. My leader will either give me the solution verbatim from the start or better the idea I have.

In the long term this creates a cycle whereby team members don't need to think any more as my leader does all the work. But often this translates into apathy and frustration as individuals are not given the opportunity to learn and utilize their ideas. Active disengagement is likely to follow.

The alternative to suggesting is good coaching. It will take longer and needs some patience as the team member starts to gather experience – but their learning cycles are high. In the longer term it means that the team member is far more self-sufficient and develops the ability to think deeply and become more curious about the way things work. As this environment of learning continues individuals draw from their learned experiences to make good decisions. Leaders on the other hand who can delegate effectively move away from the minutiae and into longer term thinking and the ongoing support of organizational culture. Below we give examples of where leaders may believe they are coaching but in fact they are suggesting:

Questions like

> Have you thought about doing this?
>
> Did you speak to Sara about that?
>
> I think we need to carry it out like this, wouldn't you agree?

Often managers believe they are asking questions, but back to the ask, tell suggest model, actually quite often many of their questions fall into tell or suggest voices.

Equally there are challenges, that leaders think are questions, which can also throw the recipient off course.

While coaching is an important skill set, a given approach to a conversation is determined by the individual or team in front of us. In the circumstances of beginner or learner my role as Instructor or Mentor will require directive conversation. Or, as a mentor, I may need to share personal experiences and suggest possible courses of action to be considered. By contrast, as an individual or a team develops in their capability, my role as a true coach is skillful inquiry allowing the individual or team to find their own solutions. While as delegator my role is to listen and get out of the way!

It is repeated use of a particular style of questioning (often the wrong type) which starts to drive the wrong behaviors.

7.13. Case Study

The purposeful and effective use of our language and our attentiveness to response creates a process which we refer to as acoustic management. The following case study is a common scenario.

Using VoicePrint to improve morning meeting traction and team performance at a granular level

The success of a tiered management system relies heavily on the ability of a team to have effective dialogue – creating a safe environment to surface and explore issues, challenging the status quo and being able to set clear actions for follow up. The following case study outlines a team that was finding it difficult to get traction.

It was evident that the cross-functional morning meeting was struggling to get any real traction. On observation, the conversations lacked any kind of bite. A number of issues were presenting themselves.

- an inability to make linkages with KPIs especially where input metrics were showing green but performance was on red or vice versa
- a passive reaction to non-completion of tasks and actions or missing information
- apathy to repeating issues
- excuses accepted for poor performance with no follow up or challenge
- several members of the team as passive attendees

A typical conversation would run like this;

Supervisor: "downtime of line 3 was at 37 minutes, why?"

Team leader:	"we waited for the first product but it wasn't available so we decided to swap to the next one on the plan but that was poor quality so we had to wait for QC to put it on hold and take it off line then we needed to do a big tool change to get onto the third product"
Supervisor:	"was it product X up first?"
Team Leader:	"yes"
Supervisor:	"wasn't that a problem this morning as well?"
Team Leader:	"er, yes, but that's because there's not enough stock we're waiting for another delivery"
Supervisor:	"why wasn't it ready yesterday?"
Purchasing:	"it was due on the night shift so should have been ready"
Stores:	"it didn't arrive until after shift started yesterday"
Planning:	"it was showing there was stock on the system for the order"
Stores:	"there was no release on the pick notes last night so I don't think there was enough stock"
Supervisor:	"so it was late for yesterday but we still produced and hit plan, right? Is today's here now and is it on the plan or will we miss delivery?

Team Leader:	"yes we hit plan yesterday and I think we'll be ok for today as long as delivery comes before midday"
Planning:	"can someone tell me when the stock is arriving so I can adjust the plan"
Supervisor:	"purchasing can you make sure stock is here for today's orders and let everyone know. Will we be ok for tomorrow?
Purchasing:	"it should be here as we speak, I'll check after the meeting, there should be enough for today and tomorrow"
Supervisor:	"ok cost per kilo performance is down for that line, is that all due to the downtime?"
Line Leader:	"yes I think so"
Supervisor:	"ok let's move on..."

Nearly every meeting I attended seemed to conform to the same pattern of conversation – with the real issues not really being investigated and just firefighting the here and now.

A short VoicePrint programme was undertaken by the team exploring the implications and outcomes of using the three main voice styles of Ask/Explore, Suggest/Position and Tell/Direct and the nuances available through their associated voices.

We played back the dialogue above and started to explore which style of conversation this dialogue focused on and the effect the nature of the conversation had on the thinking and feeling of the team. We went on afterwards to analyze the conversations we *could* have had and what might have been the outcomes of doing so.

In the first instance the team thought that the conversation was based around "Explore".

In practice teams often struggle to recognize the difference between challenge and inquiry in the initial days of analyzing their dialogue. One of the common mistakes made is hearing anything with a questioning form or tone as necessarily an "Explore or ask" and not recognizing that challenges themselves can often come in the form of a question; the presence of a question mark is not the singular marker of an inquiry! Helping the team understand the real nuance between challenge and inquiry can often be a real unlock moment in improving dialogue, along with creating better awareness of the unskillful use of these voices – attack and interrogate.

If the dialogue was based around "Ask" and good inquiry (based on predictable outcomes) the team should feel engaged and respected. At the time of the meeting there was very little reaction around the room but away from the environment the reflective reaction to the conversation in front of them was very different:

- **Frustration** from the supervisor that this is a relatively common and ongoing issue and nobody from the wider team is taking responsibility for it.
- **Stress** from the team leader about how to respond as the issue has happened time and time again but that he was trying his best to hit plan
- **Irritation** from the planner that this sort of issue takes up a lot of her time adjusting the plan and **confusion** as to why the first product wasn't available as the system indicated plenty of stock
- **Relief** from the QA team that the product quality issue had been picked up before getting to the customer but **disappointment** that the second product had been pulled

to line out of order before they could do their verification checks

- **Annoyance** from the purchasing team that the first product couldn't be found as there were no stock issues and that product had not been handled properly resulting in quality issues

- **Worry** from the store man that perhaps there was a mistake in booking first product stock but **relieved** to have got away without being questioned!

- **Reticence** from the rest of the team about offering an opinion in case they'd done something wrong

- **Dejection** from engineering that nobody seemed bothered about the disruption to his team's plan for the day with yet another ASAP tool change

If the team were all feeling like this, why did nobody express this in the meeting? And what are the voices that are being used that are making us feel this way?

On closer inspection of the dialogue, the team agreed that most of the questions that get asked in their meetings are closer to challenge than inquire and that in many cases the challenges are not very skillful and often feel like attack which in turn switches the team off from engaging in lengthy dialogue for fear of coming under more fire! They agreed that they spend very little time properly asking questions, truly exploring, to understand the issues and are more interested in giving someone something to go and sort out in the immediate moment. Most of the team stand in the shadows unless they are actually asked a question because challenge (an unskillful version of attack) is uncomfortable.

Agreeing that there had to be a better and safer way of having difficult conversations, the team agreed to break down the example conversation and think of other ways of having a similar conversation in order to achieve better outcomes.

Analyzing the first statement we sought to understand what was really important in the downtime metric, what behaviors or outcomes did we need to drive and therefore what was the dialogue that was required?

The team agreed that downtime was uncomfortable as a measure, as it indicates something is wrong, but, if we could behave well in acknowledging the root cause, it would be a really helpful issue to fix (for the whole team!) If we could embrace a problem and see it as an opportunity to do something better next time, we could get excited about fixing it for real. Managing by facts and not opinions and truly understanding the problems would be key, which meant a conscious effort to keep neutral and curious with a high level of patience! The team agreed on trying to find language that was helpful to behavior offering support and to minimize unhelpful dialogue that creates defensive behavior.

By understanding a little more of each voice in the Tell, Ask, Suggest triangle, the team started to quickly pick up the nuance of each voice and became much more aware of their body language or responses to their team members.

It took a little time to start to ask really good questions that got under the skin of the issues, but we found in general it was a skill that many of the team possessed and we could quickly start to get to root cause of issues. What we found was the biggest issue was holding people to account in completing actions; the tell voices were really weak and the team in general were not comfortable delivering these voices or being dealt them!

Challenge was still a tricky voice to use well without it being seen as an attack on an individual, particularly where repeat problems or inaction was evident. *"Why don't you have the information?"*

was often met with a roll of the eyes or an exasperated sigh and a feeling that it was so unnecessary

We deployed small subset questions to help with this by probing the problem more deeply:

> "Why is getting the information so difficult for you? What help do you need?"
>
> "Help me understand what is unreasonable in my request for the information?"
>
> "Do you understand why the information is so critical?"

The team quickly found that their inability to articulate or evaluate their reasons why caused problems in the challenge arena and when they articulated things well, challenges were much better received. The more standards were defined the easier the correct voice was to use and accept.

We took time in each team meeting to check in on how people were feeling with their new ways of talking – where an over-zealous challenge would emerge *"why did you do that?"* followed by a defensive response – we would stop the conversation and explore better ways of challenging that were less forceful but still got the desired effect.

Within a few weeks, the conversations in the team meeting were much more productive – much better team dynamics and understanding of each department's pressures, more offered solutions and coming forward with issues from the shadows in the background.

When implementing daily review meetings within a tiered management system, it is evident that the culture of the organization comes through strongly in the nature of conversations being held.

7.14. Pulling it together:

Developing leadership skills around how to effectively interact with teams is a basis for transformative participation. Asking the right questions at the right time in the right way shows that leaders are interested, and colleagues' opinions are respected. Challenging situations in the right way, that is not personal or attacking and is rooted in process conversations about issues rather than 'who', creates an environment of respect and accountability that is aligned to the objectives of the whole organization. Creating this safe learning environment is at the heart of participative transformation and is a foundation of deep excellence.

As leaders we must recognize that we have an impact through our use of dialogue with every conversation we have – getting it right provides results – getting it wrong (consistently) destroys relationships and starts to potentially drive suboptimal culture and behaviors within the organization.

If managers don't get the "open and curious" inquiry quite right, opting instead for questions that are, in fact, suggestions – we are likely to miss many opportunities for developing and engaging our staff.

Recognizing the requirement for the right dialogue in the right situation and within defined systems starts to unlock the potential of both leaders and staff alike.

We see and hear good leadership in the quality of their dialogue with individuals and teams. Good dialogue results in strong confident resilient mindsets. Good mindsets enable the right behaviors that are aligned to an open supportive and challenging culture that is the basis for deep excellence.

8 Maturity assessments and roadmaps

'The stone age didn't end because we ran out of stone. We just learned how to do things better!'

-Anon

The beginning of any journey, unless you are Alice in Wonderland, begins with knowing where you are and where you want to be.

I am always struck by the openness of some businesses to share their learning with other companies as benchmark sites for excellence. This can be a great learning experience for business executives, but there is a risk that the experience is too shallow. We can see tools easily, and, if we know what we are looking for, we can see and hear good or bad behaviors. However, it takes more time than any benchmark visit normally allows to understand how business systems work together to enable deep excellence.

The way you need systems to integrate is very often unique to your business. The specific behaviors your organization needs for long-term sustainable excellence are unique to the essence of what your business is about. You can't copy any of this. You must discover what excellence means for you and understand how far away from it you currently are.

An internal current state assessment activity which reaches across all aspects of your business is the best way to begin your journey. Sometimes it is possible to use hard performance figures to compare your current state to same or similar industries. Metrics such as lead-times, inventory turns, stock holding value versus sales, customer satisfaction rates are all interesting numbers, but in the early days of any transformation journey we need to go deeper than this.

We need to understand how well work works in the business. We need to understand how good we are at improving work in a way that is impactful to the bottom line. Most importantly, we need to engage in real open conversations about the current state, culture, behaviors and systems behind the levels of performance we currently observe.

Once we have a true reflection of where we are – our level of maturity – on our journey to deep excellence, only then, can we begin to put a realistic roadmap in place to move forward.

The first section of this chapter details our approach to Maturity Assessment and developing a Roadmap. Our approach is based on our international consulting practice and client engagement over the last thirty years. Before we explain the assessment activity let's refresh some core thinking behind our approach.

8.1. *What are we looking for in a benchmark assessment?*

The whole concept of systemic improvement has its origins in the Lean Principles. The principles themselves are a set of guidelines for creating a system of improvement within your organization. Understand what your customer wants, understand how you create these wants, continually remove non-value-adding activity (waste), run your process at the speed of the customer, and then continually improve what you do. Pretty simple stuff but very powerful when applied properly and systemically across a business. This approach is still the basis for all improvement.

Specify value from the perspective of the customer	What do our customers want?
Identify the value stream	How do we ensure everything we do matches what the customer wants and is willing to pay for?
Make the value creating steps flow...	How do we do what the customer wants without delay?
... at the pull of the customer	How do we deliver what the customer wants at their pace?
Strive for perfection	How do we continually improve the service to our customers?

We are all aware of its flaws in the principles in that it lacks a strong people dimension. Countless leadership and coaching publications enjoy highlighting this, but this is simply down to how the principles are interpreted.

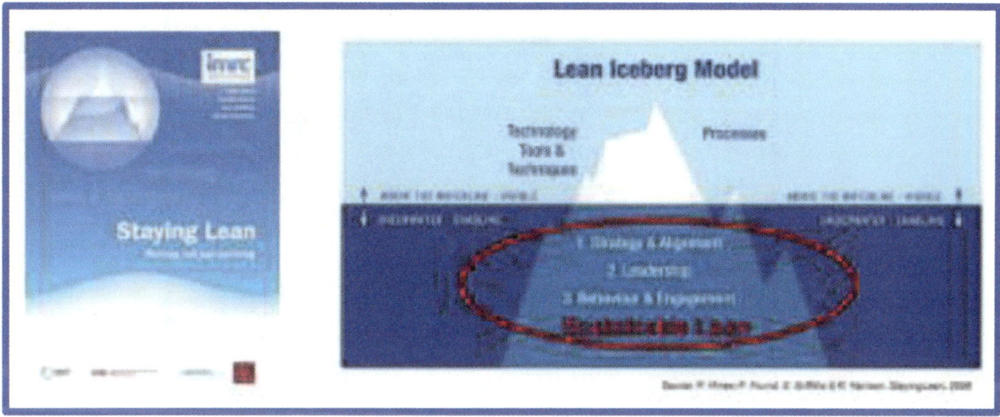

Figure 37: Staying Lean Thriving Not Just Surviving (Hines et al., 2008) and the Iceberg Model © S A Partners

In the publication *Staying Lean* we introduced the concept of the Lean Iceberg which highlights the need for leadership and strategy systems to support the application of Lean Thinking. This brings into focus the need for both 'above and below the waterline activities' (Hines et al., 2008).

This Shingo Award winning book revolutionized how we and other organizations look at organizations. The publication introduced the Lean Business Model which was originally used as a basis for our assessments and roadmaps. These assessments looked at each dimension of the Lean Business Model and assessed the maturity around pre-defined features and systems within a business.

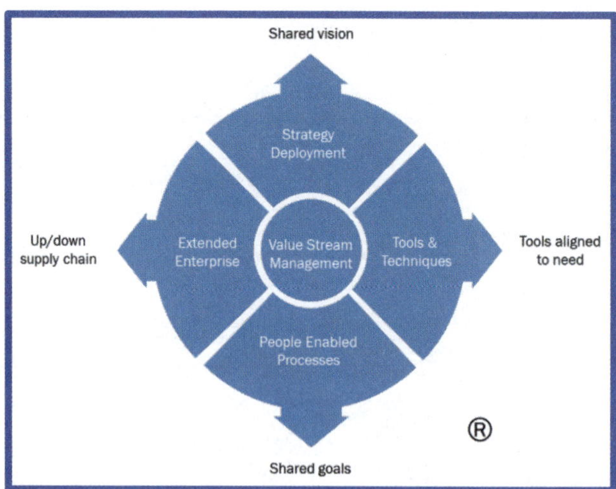

Figure 38: The Original Lean Business Model © S A Partners.

During the early days of the Lean Business Model an intervention with Whirlpool led to an additional piece of thinking developed by Chris Craycraft of Whirlpool Global Continuous Improvement team. Chris analysed the effectiveness of Lean Implementation in two different plants, one who adopted a Kaizen Blitz approach and one who adopted a strategic lean approach. The results showed Kaizen has its place and it can deliver improvement but it's unlikely to sustain without the appropriate leadership, cultural and strategic infrastructure to sustain it.

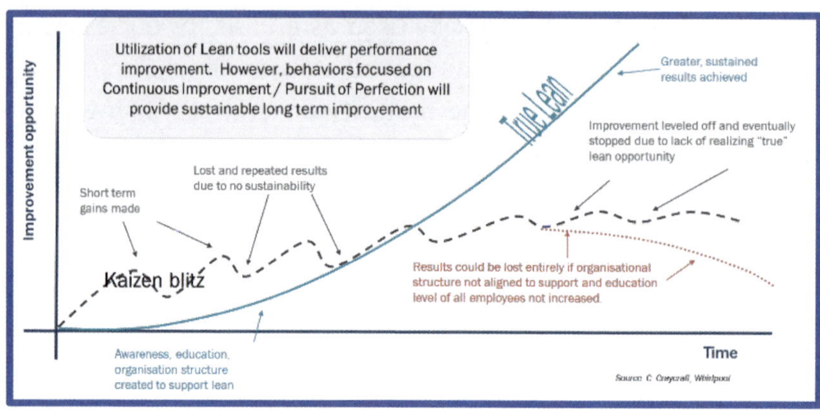

Figure 38 Chris Craycraft Sustainable Lean versus Kaizen Lean

The Shingo Institute refined and developed its thinking around systems, behaviors and ten guiding principles to support the application of the "Shingo Model" of enterprise excellence. The Shingo Model brings into sharp focus the need for supportive humble leadership styles as a foundation for sustainable enterprise excellence. The model also crystalized thinking around key business systems and behaviors and how core system must support the expression of ideal behaviors throughout the enterprise.

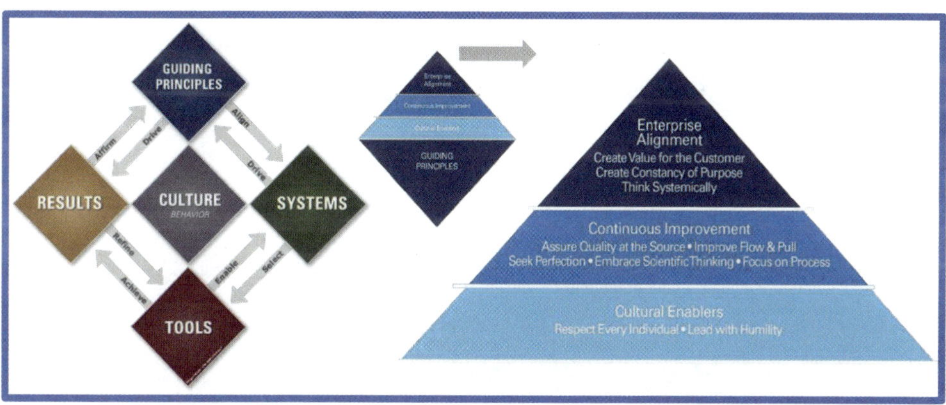

Figure 39: The Shingo Model of Enterprise Excellence (Shingo, 2022)

8.2. Our current approach to maturity assessments.

Against the backdrop outlined above S A Partners have developed the following three models to help guide organizations through the assessment and roadmap process. The three elements consist of our Enterprise Excellence Model, the infamous 'Squiggly Curve', and Systems Alignment.

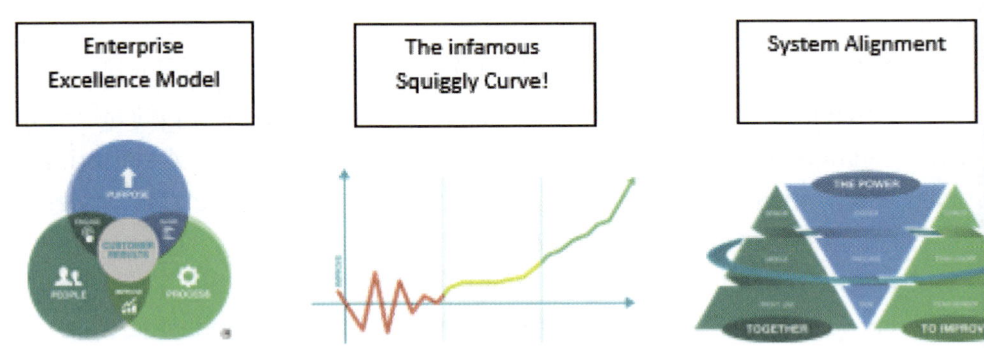

Figure 40: S A Partners Transformation models © S A Partners.

8.3. Enterprise Excellence Model

The Enterprise Excellence Model links the needs of customers with a defined organizational purpose. The performance of the organization is optimized by aligning systems, processes, and tasks with engaged people at all levels who are focused on continually improving what they do every day.

The key feature of the model is how each of the systems within each element work together to support the effective implementation of Sustainable Enterprise Excellence. It's not about being exceptional in one element – it is about the balance of seven areas working together to create an organizational culture of deep excellence.

Successful organizations believe in both their people and their process. These organizations recognize the strengths and weaknesses of the human condition. They tap into the best of the human condition: willingness to improve and be a part of something, to address our normal human weaknesses.

Successful organizations have a key focus on the intersecting areas of align, engage, and improve. These areas contain key signature systems that form the glue of deep excellence. The tiered management system, the improvement system, the leadership systems, the strategy deployment and communication systems, and the system by which we develop skills within the organization.

8.4. Letting the processes speak to you

Improvement activities happen when processes 'cry out' to be improved. Trends of Key Performance Indicators (KPIs), alarm histories, breakdown, customer satisfaction measures, are all wonderful precious sources of information during an assessment. They all represent the voice of our processes. Asking simple leading questions such as, Is today a good day or a bad day? Is this week a good week or a bad week? Based on the answer we ask, *'so what tells you how you are doing and what has performance looked like over the last three months?'* These questions can be asked at any level and in any part of the organization. In the answer we look for the connection to the voice of the process.

Great things happen when team members discover the voices of their process. They begin to discover and understand the levers or leading indicators which – if managed or resolved – prevent poor performance and frustration around the work that needs to be done.

They find solutions to problems and new ways to improve what they do. They feel a connection, they learn. They own the solutions, and have a new story to tell around persistence, ingenuity and achievement. They bring their hands, head and heart to work every day.

Below we outline four insights or learning around our use of the Enterprise Excellence Model in our Maturity Assessment work.

Insight 1.- Balance Your Efforts

In order to achieve sustainable customer results, we need to balance our efforts in how we align our processes with how we engage our people. Too many organizations spend way too much time driving process conformance and nowhere near enough time working with their people.

Insight 2.- Focus on the Intersects

Most organizations have well defined processes, a strategy of sorts and some form of people management system. The great organizations focus on how these interact with each other and how more importantly they delivered what their customers need.

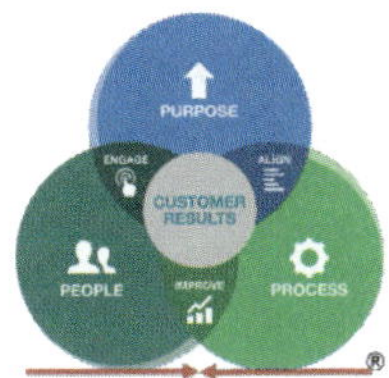

Insight 3.- Improvement Two Ways

Improvement can happen when buzzers, alarms, targets and measures tell us to fix things - we can design an improvement system and mandate our people to follow it: process-driven. How about we engage and enthuse our people so that they come up with great ways of improving what they do: unprompted people-driven.

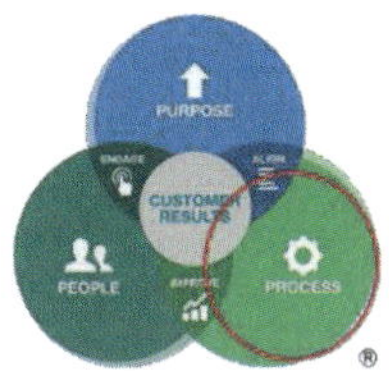

Insight 4.- Slaves to the Process

Organizations often approach what they do by taking what they did last year and improving it by 5%, so a capacity budget to utilise all its assets. Sustainable success is achieved by building the organization around the needs of the customer, developing a sustainable purpose, aligning its processes, engaging its people to continually improve what it does.

Figure 41: Our team at S A Partners' insights from the application of Enterprise Excellence Assessment Model © S A Partners.

8.5. *The Enterprise Excellence Journey – The Squiggly line!*

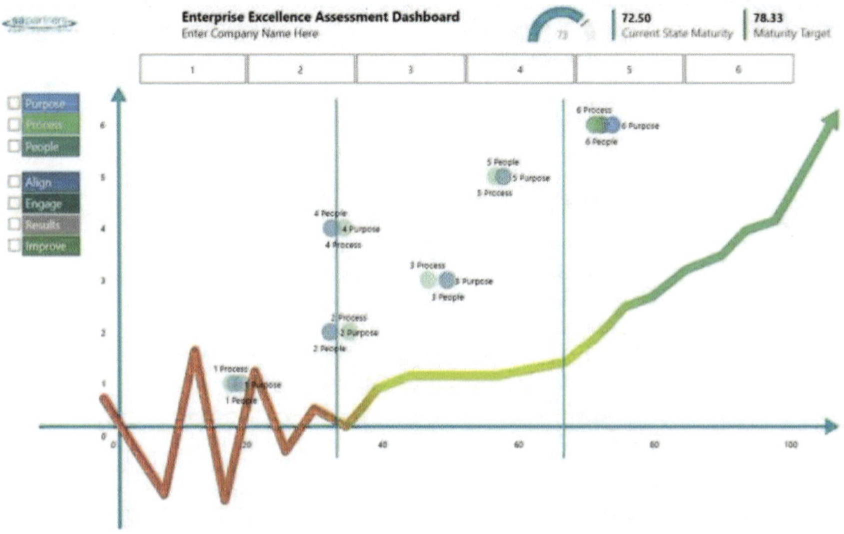

Figure 42: The 'Squiggly Line' journey to Sustainable Enterprise Excellence © S A Partners

The Enterprise Excellence Journey when combined with the Enterprise Excellence Model helps organizations understand maturity and develop solutions that are appropriate based on the ambitions of the organization. It defines the style of leadership required to move onto the next level of improvement. We have tried to call it many things: the Enterprise Excellence Journey is the formal name, but somehow it always becomes the squiggly line!

The image is a powerful one. It can drive strong and deep conversations about what it feels like to be in the red zone, and what teams could aspire to in the green zone. On one occasion, I asked a senior leadership team to define where they were on the 'squiggly line' before we completed the maturity assessment. The senior leader did not hesitate in stating his thoughts that the site was firmly in the middle of the yellow stability zone.

As he spoke, I could see the faces of his peers describe a different world! Some heads went down, some faces winced, some eyes went to heaven. All of which went unseen by the leader!

Following the assessment, the discussion and feedback placed the site in left of the middle of the red zone. The leader was surprised at this feedback, however the discussion that followed was one of the most open and frank conversations the leadership team had with their leader.

> "You are never here, how can you understand what is really going on? You are rarely seen on the shop floor? You know we have had consistent issues so how can you believe we are stable? We are constantly bringing in new immature products that do not achieve predicted quality or productivity rates. Our teams must deal with this and deliver on their standard product portfolio?"

Equally, the leader had questions: "So why don't we talk about the reality? We have a meeting structure why are we not able to manage issues at the right level?"

The conversation went on for the rest of the afternoon. It was transformational. The false mirror was broken. The team could now focus on the reality and piece by piece work together to win back the trust of the frontline teams to help them fix it.

The phases of the journey are largely self-explanatory, but the powerful open conversations they can provoke never cease to amaze us.

In the following section we Look at the zones of the 'squiggly line' and how to move through them.

8.6. Red zone

If you find yourself in the red reactive area it is a place to regain control and re-define or define systems of work. The leadership approach is to promote stability by defining business systems and creating standards, it is likely to be an instructional, mentoring environment where standards need to be developed and individuals trained and mentored through to the consistent efficient use and improvement of these standards. The pursuit and visualisation of stability is all important as this will provide the platform for further improvement. In the red zone the focus is on engagement of the team in what needs to be done and why.

8.7. Yellow zone

Should an organization find itself in the yellow proactive phase (a very rare and happy feeling) the leadership approach is to promote velocity and improvement, if the standards are in place and working well, the focus is to improve what's being done. The leadership style here is more towards a mentoring and coaching approach where we invest in the knowledge of the people and ensure they own what is happening. In the yellow zone we continue to confirm and manage engagement, but we balance that with ensuring the energy we have released through engagement is aligned with what is important for the business.

8.8. Green zone – moving to deep excellence

Finally, there are very few organizations that exist in the green excellence phase: here the leadership approach is to promote agility and innovation. The leadership approach moves towards coaching and delegating – encouraging people to fully control and improve what they do. The organization can adapt and move quickly to the needs of the customer. In the green zone there is an even greater emphasis on engagement and reduced emphasis on alignment. The business knows where it is going and why. Constant communication and recognition of the appropriate behaviors is key. For these companies there is nothing they can't achieve by working together.

The focus on observable behaviors is consistent throughout the journey to deep excellence. However, what we look for and who we look at and listen to will vary as we move along the line. In the red zone we often see low levels of management and supervisor skills at all levels but particularly in frontline management and supervisor teams. Here, a stake often needs to be placed in the ground around what are acceptable and unacceptable behaviors. We may need to focus on driving out fear, on stopping the blame game and finger pointing. Trust between teams may have been lost. Here lies the real contact sport for the senior leadership team. The behaviors observed on the frontline are often a reflection of the shadow cast by the behaviors of the leadership team. To move from the red zone there is a huge focus on modifying what are often the contributory behaviors of the leadership team.

Adopting the wrong approach to discussion around behaviors will have the opposite effect on the change we desire. As leaders we need to ensure our people are aware of leadership style changes; don't do this by stealth: adopt a position of humility, admit what was wrong, and draw a line in the sand. Leaders must promote and champion the agreed behaviors or ways of working together as one team.

The following diagrams help us define impactful approaches to improvement during benchmark assessments.

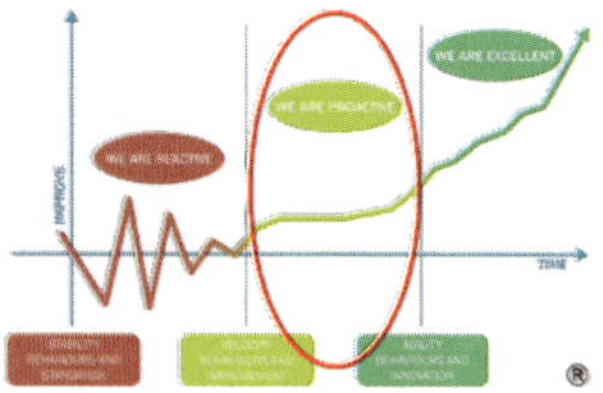

Insight 1.- Stability First-

Stability is exciting, stability ensures what you think should happen will happen; people like stability - it calms them, they know what's happening, it gives people a sense of control and safety. Too many organizations crave blue-sky magic fixes, but all fancy tower blocks have to be built on firm foundations. You cannot customise until you have standardised.

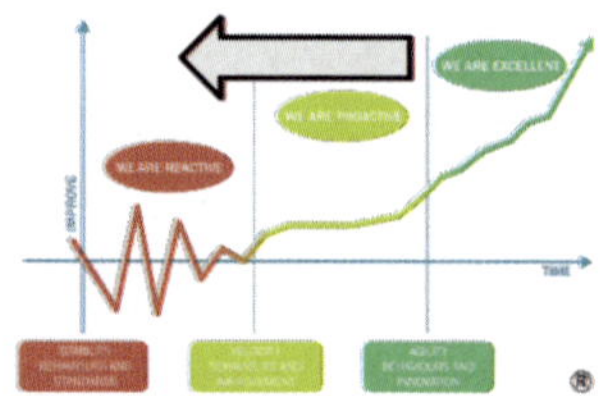

Insight 2.- Sustain

Remember you can go backwards quicker than you can go forwards. Change happens all the time and can come at you from all angles. Ensure you have locked in your gains with robust systems and routines that prevent slippage and ensure you learn from what you do. Don't become complacent about your improvement journey.

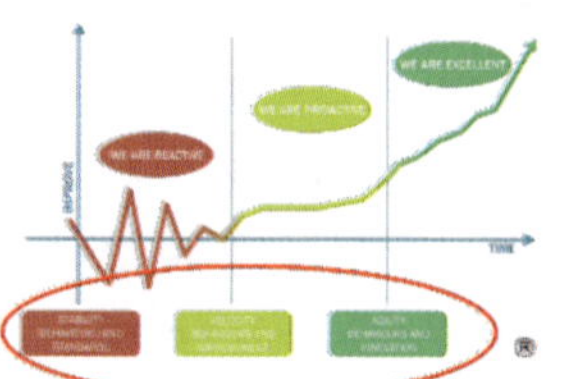

Insight 3.- Ideal Behaviour

Understand where you are as an organization. Don't kid yourself with false data or ego, be honest and adapt your leadership style to the environment you are in or the organization you want to be. Stabilise what you do by using the appropriate style of leadership and then work with your people and systems using the appropriate leading behaviors to deliver it.

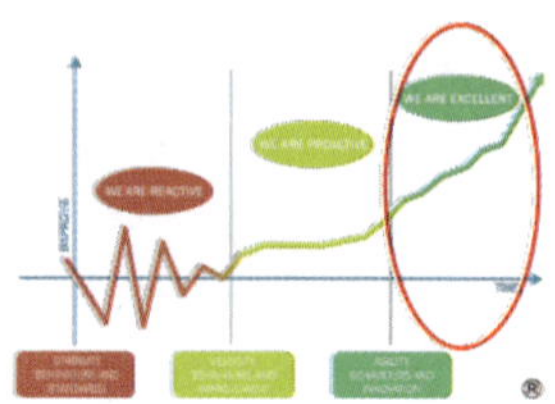

Insight 4.- Manage the programme

"We are excellent." Everybody wants to be there; unfortunately, very few people are there. It's assumed to be a system and process path but really its more about engaged people working in an aligned workplace. Change and improvement happen consistently but people embrace it and become part of it. It is seen as part of the work and not something that is done to people.

Figure 43: The S A Partners team's insights on the journey to excellence © S A Partners

8.9. Maturity of leadership style

As previously discussed, leadership style is constantly developing and maturing as organizations move along their transformation journey. As leadership skills develop, deliberate choices in the use of language are made when dealing with each phase of the journey. In the red reactive phase promoting stability, standardisation and having alignment conversations around defined standards are crucial. Conformance and clarity conversations are commonplace. The language used will primarily be an instructional, mentoring style focussing on telling and suggesting.

As organizations move to the proactive phase, we promote velocity and improvement, through mentoring and coaching by balancing alignment and engagement conversations and focussing on suggesting and asking.

With the green excellent phase, leaders promote agility and innovation by coaching and delegating – primarily through asking and listening. It goes without saying that, within the green zone, the right conversations are happening at the right time and in the right place throughout the organization. We see evidence of quality leadership and coaching at all levels. Offers are often made to develop these skills to enable improvement journeys within external suppliers or community groups.

8.10. What we look for

During our maturity assessments we consistently look for evidence of four key activities within the organization:

- A commitment to developing leadership at all levels
- Focus on defining, creating, and improving the necessary systems
- Well-defined processes and tasks to deliver the needs of the organization
- Creating improvement capability at all levels with a management system to ensure success.

What's critical about successful improvement is the balance between each of these elements. Don't create improvement coaches, if you haven't developed the processes, systems, and tasks for them to work on. Don't expect leaders to lead, if they don't know how to. Finally, don't expect improvement programme activity to deliver itself. You need a system to prioritise, align and manage the execution of these projects.

8.11. Looking for maturity in systems thinking

Systems, as we mentioned in previous chapters, are the architecture of any business. They create the framework for people to work within. These systems may be formal or informal, but they are there. It is best that they are formally defined and described to support and enable desired behaviors to ensure sustainable excellence.

Systems, and the processes and tasks they consist of, can be applied at the organization level or departmental level. We can have a system that defines how people enter, contribute and retire from an organization: the people management system. Or, we can think about the system by which the warehouse operates receiving and storing raw material, and shipping finished products. Both systems consist of workflows, processes and tasks that make them work consistently. Few companies, however, actually create a document that describes these systems and how they integrate with other systems at a high level.

8.12. Systems thinking what we look for

Our simple system model reminds us that no one system or group of systems can stand alone. Remove any of the supporting triangles in the model below and the structure becomes unstable. The model was built based on our belief at S A Partners that transformation and improvement occurs by people working together within a defined system of work and who are constantly focused on improving those systems of work. *Together the power to improve.*

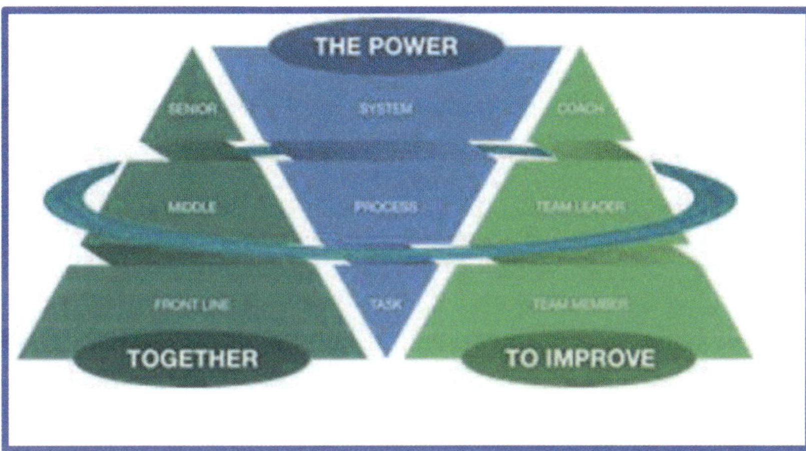

Figure 44: Core System Elements Supporting any Journey to Enterprise Excellence © S A Partners

The systems model has four elements:

The Power:

These are the core systems that make the business work. How we develop and deploy strategy. How we deliver the service or products we sell. How we develop and improve skills. We look for structure and definition around these systems, particularly the signature systems of strategy deployment and key work systems.

Together:

These are the systems that align and engage teams in the culture and purpose of the organization. They include systems by which we develop leadership skills at all levels. It can also include communication systems and systems by which the organization defines, deploys and monitors culture and behaviors.

Improve:

How we develop skills at all levels to drive improvement everywhere, every day, which is aligned to the strategic needs of the business.

The Blue Ring:

This represents the system and discipline to prioritize and manage project and programme execution at every level.

Not only do we review the core systems, we must also review how these systems integrate between each of the triangles. For example, Leader standard work provides a powerful integration activity between strategy deployment and leadership skills. Similarly, continuous improvement provides the essential link between strategy deployment, work systems and improvement skills.

8.13. Five essential system elements of a successful transformation programme

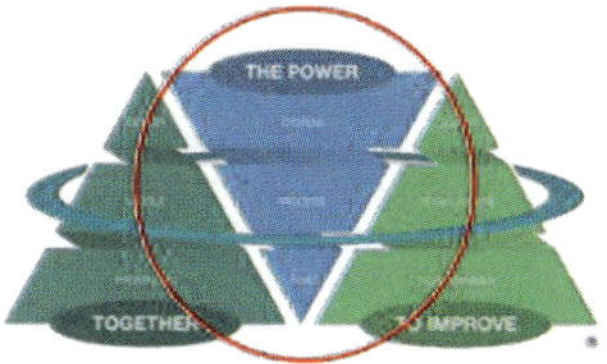

Insight 1.-Set the goals

Bottom up or top down? The answer is both, in order for effective improvement to happen in an organization we need to create an integrated set of systems, processes and tasks. These elements need to combine to provide timely accurate deployment, escalation and cross-functional working to deliver dynamic improvement at all levels.

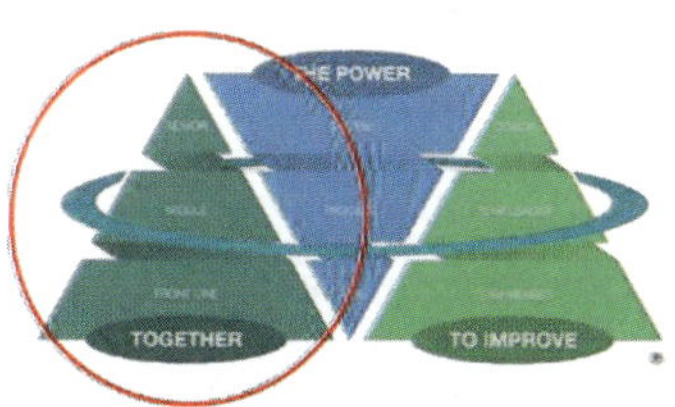

Insight 2.-Manage the journey

Leaders at all levels need to understand what is required of themselves and their reports, be fully self-aware and equipped with tools of delegation, coaching, mentoring and instruction, to enable them to maximise the potential of their teams. They should operate in a Leader Standard Work System that defines how and when the organization delivers its goals.

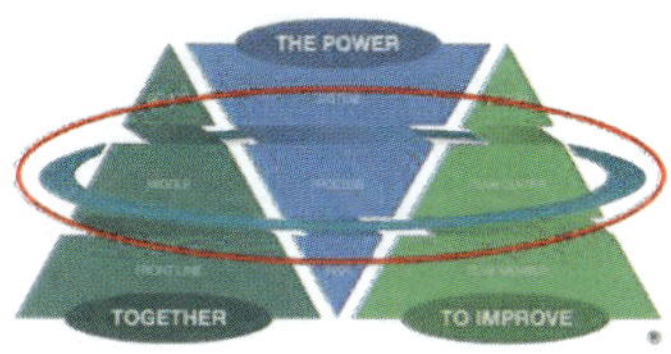

Insight 3.-Improve what you do

Improvement is a way of life, but it's not that easy as people are not always equipped with the appropriate skills and confidence to improve what they do. Developing common skills at all levels -system, process and task is critical in delivering improvement. Focus on Purpose, Process and most importantly people to deliver sustainable results

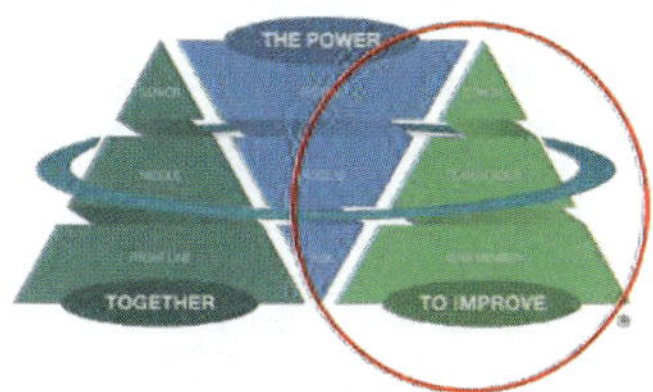

Insight 4.-Manage the programme

"You get what you measure" so to deliver sustainable improvement we need to measure what we do and manage our programme of work. Don't be ashamed of benefits but focus on a balance of measures which are both delivery focussed such as customer, cost and compliance, supported by enabling measures such as colleagues, capacity and capability. Apply PDCA!

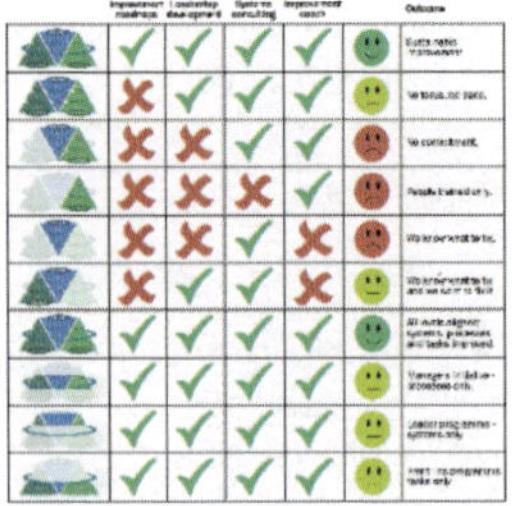

Insight 5.-Balance is key

For true sustainable improvement to happen we need to develop a change programme that defines how leaders operate at all levels work with their people, to deliver the critical organization systems, processes and tasks, whilst ensuring people at all levels understand what is expected of them and have the skills to improve what they do.

Create a programme that works for the organization and ensure the sequence of the plan is best aligned to the circumstances the organization finds itself in. Remember this plan may need to be fluid, change is very unlikely to travel in a straight line so be prepared for some bumps and turns in the road ahead.

8.14. Roadmaps

Roadmaps can take many forms and there are numerous IT packages available to help track progress. Our advice is to keep it simple, keep it visual, keep it front and centre of the organization's activity.

Ensure change is integrated with people's roles and performance objectives. Make change part of the job don't make it something that can be done when we have time. Make the time. Review and eliminate non-value-adding meetings, carve out improvement time in the plan, hire temporary or permanent backfill. Whatever you do commit to giving your team the time to make things better. This is often the first hurdle for programmes to fall at.

A central plan and forum must be established that is visited at least monthly by the key players. Four box updates from each of the significant work packages provide a simple effective framework once we are taking a deep dive into each at a regular interval. Don't treat the maturity assessment as a one off. Revisit it at least annually to track progress.

The appointment of a Master coach early on was essential, the development of strategy, highlighting of key projects, training people at the right time and management of improvement all needed sequencing. The simple horizons tool shown below is a useful tool to help sequence implementation planning.

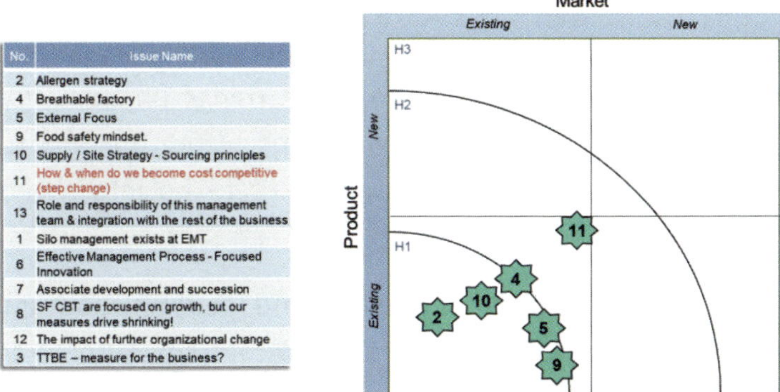

No.	Issue Name
2	Allergen strategy
4	Breathable factory
5	External Focus
9	Food safety mindset.
10	Supply / Site Strategy - Sourcing principles
11	How & when do we become cost competitive (step change)
13	Role and responsibility of this management team & integration with the rest of the business
1	Silo management exists at EMT
6	Effective Management Process - Focused Innovation
7	Associate development and succession
8	SF CBT are focused on growth, but our measures drive shrinking!
12	The impact of further organizational change
3	TTBE – measure for the business?

Setting Priorities and Horizons © S A Partners.

8.15. In practice

So that's some of the theory, but in practice what do you do. We see far too many organizations buying an assessment tool, giving it to the CI guy and telling them to build a roadmap. Invariably this doesn't work. Success happens when we align all the team around what we are trying to do – we all agree initially on the WHY.

Our first step during any maturity assessment is to bring the senior team together and have everyone "level up" on where they think the organization is – how its systems, processes and tasks are performing and, more importantly, where they feel the organization is behaviourally and what the key challenges are.

We often begin with a simple desk top assessment with the leadership team as an aid to open up and provoke conversation. A free Micro assessment is available at www.sapartners .com for you to try within your own team.

Producing detailed plans here is not critical, its more about bringing people together and developing a common aim; it's about facilitation and conversations. What's critical here is the assessment is designed to provoke continuous improvement mindset and to emphasize why that mindset is so important for the business. Things will change. The scale and pace is down to the ambition of the team, but rest assured things will change. The leadership team need to be ready for this and be prepared for the necessary time and effort to make things happen. Conducting assessments, coming up with roadmaps, and failing to deliver improvement invariably causes improvement to go into reverse rather than move forward.

You can never underestimate the need for and focus on communication at the beginning and throughout the transformation journey. The time required to ensure people understand, absorb, align, and engage with what the programme will entail cannot be overlooked. The middle management teams are always a particularly important group to focus on as these will be the engine for change.

Communication is a two-way process. Be prepared to speak and listen and to reshape what happens next. Always ask for feedback and learn.

8.16. Moving forward with an assessment:

No progress is possible without a plan, detailing responsibilities for both conducting the assessment and communicating to the organization about what's happening. Planning and communication set the stage for a successful, engaging, current state assessment. Jumping feet first into doing, is often a recipe for disaster and can lead to programmes going into reverse and not moving forward.

During the assessment process a significant amount of time is to be spent talking to people and putting them at their ease about the process and how their feedback will be used. Trust is key. A commitment needs to be made that anything said in any interview is confidential. Any feedback will be assessed based on common themes raised through all interviews carried out. It should be impossible to identify any individual contribution to the process. It is paramount that every conversation feels safe and that team members can give their open honest feedback on their view of the current state both from process standpoint and from the organizational culture.

8.17. Assessment Software:

S A Partners assessment software allows Organizations, Business units, systems and even processes to be assessed and roadmaps produced, developing and producing integrated programmes.

The diagnostic tool first understands the Operating Model for the organization and then diagnoses performance based on how well results are being produced, how aligned activities are, how engaged people are and what potential for improvement has been created. This ensures the diagnostic examines the organization's ability to create sustainable solutions.

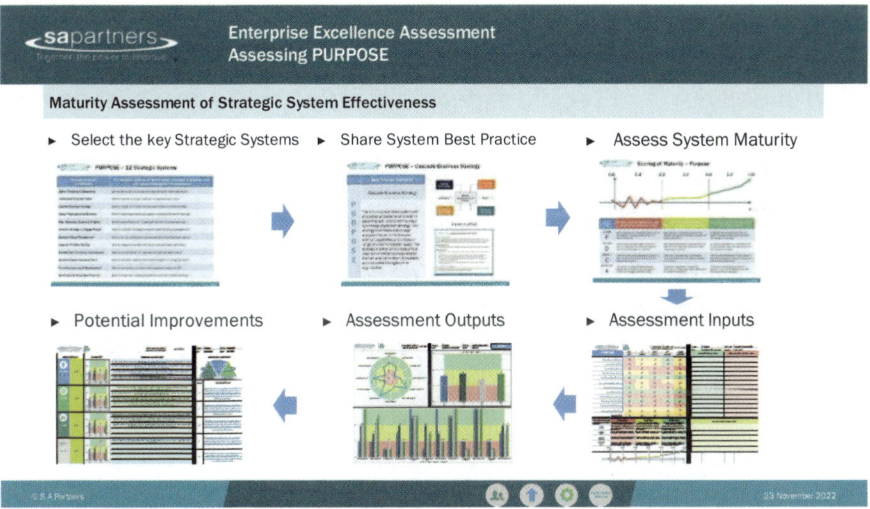

Extracts from S A Partners Enterprise Excellence Benchmark Assessment software tool © S A Partners

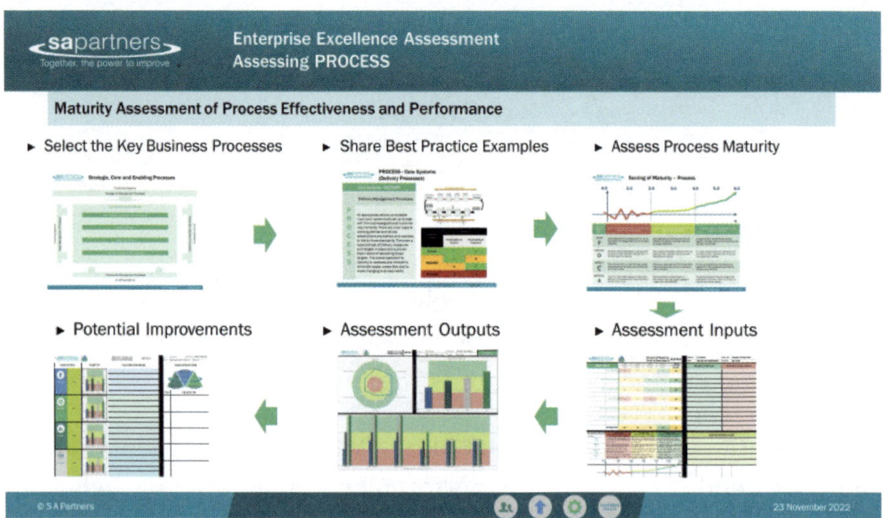

Extracts from S A Partners Enterprise Excellence Benchmark Assessment software tool © S A Partners.

On completion of the diagnostic(s), it is critical the results are shared with the leadership team of the business and actions and projects are then created via discussion and understanding. All too often solutions are created in isolation and people expected to deliver change whilst doing the day job. We need to work out what is urgent, what can be done, what capacity is available, what the risks, issues and dependencies of the programme are, the reality of the situation! Too often leadership teams are delusional and will hear what they want to hear. Get some data and some facts and do what's realistic. So, what if it takes a little longer: better to get there than not get there at all. I am sure there is an old tale of a tortoise and a hare here somewhere.

Benchmark assessment can have their limitations and comparing your organization to another is always difficult as no two organizations are the same, they each have their own drivers and culture. We recommend building your own diagnostics around your systems and analysing your culture to achieve your goals. The key is to build sustainable improvement culture to consistently delivery improved results through an engaged and aligned team.

9 The Final Chapter?

'If we have any hope of a thriving planet – much less a thriving business – 50 years from now, it is going to take all of us doing what we can with the resources we have.'

-Yvon Chouinard, founder of Patagonia

Working is not living. Living is growing your family and community relationships. It is achieving your personal goals. It is searching out and enjoying the incredible experiences our beautiful planet has to offer. Work can no doubt support our ability to achieve these things, but work is not life.

But work and workplaces can interweave with all these things and help individuals achieve their purpose. Workplaces can bring common interest and purpose within colleagues, build friendships, encourage creativity, and support lifelong learning experiences as a basis for personal growth and wellbeing. Enlightened organizations recognize and support the importance of strong collegiate relationships and personal learning journeys and actively facilitate and guide them towards a common purpose.

Inspiring individuals to be their best selves, growing personally and professionally, holding themselves accountable and contributing to something bigger than the individual can only take place in a work environment that truly reflects and functions within these values. It is now clear that individuals are expecting more from their workplaces. Not necessarily more in-terms of remuneration, rather a greater appreciation on the part of the employer that work is an enabler for a full life.

There are now more choices available in how individuals engage with work and how they work. Individuals seek work that will align to their lifestyle and goals. They seek workplaces that are vibrant and allow them to actively contribute to a genuine purpose that is meaningful to them. Such organizations are clear and confident in their purpose and constantly reinforce the way work works within the organization. They speak to their purpose and openly reflect on it in the decisions that they make on the path ahead. For the employee it is a purpose that is real, impactful, and positive.

To expect an individual to work and flourish in an organization that is wasteful, inefficient, bureaucratic, and overly complex with a culture that is dogmatic inflexible or even toxic, is unrealistic. Even if these businesses are highly profitable and make the right noises as regards inclusion, improvement and social responsibility, good people soon see through the pomp and seek alternatives.

It is sad to see but unless an organization responds effectively to this situation a cycle of decline can begin. Word gets out. Good employees become harder to find. Those that land in the organization soon leave. Those that stay either work at a sub optimal level or cultivate and hide in the negative underperforming culture that exists. To bring in 'talent' the organization is forced to pay more, exacerbating the struggling profitability, and creating unrealistic expectations on what any one individual can achieve. Stress builds as key positions are not filled. Balls are dropped, quality and performance decline. New product introductions go elsewhere, and the future becomes shaky.

The only way organizations can achieve the level of deep excellence necessary for a sustainable future is to engage their teams in the development and improvement of a purposefully designed network of business systems. Systems that are fully aligned to achieve the overall purpose of the organization. Systems that are not stagnant but are constantly improved by the insights and experiences of those working in and interacting with them. Revenue profit and sales are only an enabler of that purpose not an end in themselves. Leaders within such organizations must be constantly vigilant to ensure colleagues can interact with these critical business systems in a way that supports the ideal behaviors necessary to do effective and efficient work.

Doing work in a standard repetitive way can be boring and soulless. Leaders therefore must constantly connect the achievement of good work and the improvement of that work, with individual and team learning and the overall purpose of the organization. It is an ongoing challenge for leaders who must continually hone and develop their own skills to mentor, coach and delegate effectively to enable continual learning and improvement within their teams.

This is the last chapter of this book. As we read of and experience the radical changes that are happening to our planet it is hard not to believe we are entering a last chapter of stable bountiful life on our planet. But this does not have to be the case. Where we have managed, and protected, nature has healed. Wrong can be righted.

The environmental impact of industry in all sectors is under the spotlight of legislators, NGOs and the individuals who work within them. There is no longer a moral space for waste and inefficiency. No justification for over -complexity than results in error and frustration.

When I began studying and applying Lean thinking thirty years ago, the aim was to constantly remove nonvalue add. In doing so the organization created more capacity to focus on new or greater levels of customer value to grow. However, we are now faced with a new paradigm. Endless "growth" is now a path to significant global risk. Organizations will be forced to consider new concepts of what growth means and what will be considered as "value" in the near future? Is it making more stuff to pack into landfills? Or will there be a new sense of value which can be achieved within the latent untapped capacity of every organization.

There is a new and pressing responsibility to manage the resources we have as effectively and efficiently as possible and consider new less impactful value propositions. This will require a new and greater level of enterprise-wide excellence. One that reaches through product and service design, manufacturing through to delivery, final disposal, or reuse. This level of excellence is a deep all-pervading level of excellence that is powered and sustained by the people within the organization who thrive in a culture that is actively managed and maintained by the leadership community.

As leaders, business owners and employees we hope you will play your part to ensure this is not the final chapter. As individuals with influence over the resources within your organization you now not only have the normal challenges of business activity, but you are now faced with a powerful **moral obligation** to use the resources available to you in the most effective and efficient way possible. In addition, you must constantly seek to reduce resource consumption and the wider impacts of your organization on the planet on which we live.

This is an immense challenge, but it is the new nature **in** business. You cannot do this alone. As we have discussed in this book there are fantastic people in your business looking for purpose and meaning. They are looking to improve their skills and knowledge to create better futures for themselves, their families and their communities. Bring them with you in your pursuit of real meaningful deep excellence within your organization and **make it happen**.

Thank you for taking the time to read our book.

We wish you the very best on your journey.

John, Simon, Juliette, Bryan.

Bibliography

Allen, B. R., & Bosworth, A. A. (2022). *Systems design: Building systems that drive ideal behaviors.* Routledge.

Argyris, C., Putnam, R., & McClain, D. (1985). *Action science: Concepts, methods, and skills for research and intervention.* San Francisco: Jossey-Bass.

Asch, S. E. (1951). Effects of group pressure on the modification and distortion of judgments. In H. Guetzkow (Ed.), *Groups, leadership and men: Research in human relations* (pp. 177–190). Pittsburgh: Carnegie Press.

Asch, S. E. (1955). Opinions and social pressure. *Scientific American, 193*(5), 31–35.

Barham, L., & Everett, D. (2021). Semiotics and the origin of language in the lower palaeolithic. *Journal of Archaeological Method and Theory, 28*(2), 535–579.

Charlson, R. J., Lovelock, J. E., Andreae, M., & Warren, S. (1987). Oceanic phytoplankton, atmospheric sulphur, cloud albedo and climate. *Nature, 326*(6114), 655-661.

Choi, C. Q. (2011, July). *'Invisible Gorilla' test shows how little we notice*. Retrieved from Live Science: https://www.livescience.com/6727-invisible-gorilla-test-shows-notice.html

Coolsaet, B. (2015). Transformative participation in agrobiodiversity governance: making the case for an environmental justice approach. *Journal of Agricultural and Environmental Ethics, 28*, 1089–1104.

Cosmides, L., & Tooby, J. (1997, January 13). *Evolutionary psychology: A primer.* Retrieved from Centre for Evolutionary Psychology, University of California, Santa Barbara: https://www.cep.ucsb.edu/primer.html

Csikszentmihalyi, M. (2013). *Flow: The psychology of happiness.* New York: Random House.

Cutliff, B. (2022). Slowing the great resignation: Leaders, it's time to engage! The mediating effect of psychological capital on self-leadership and work engagement. *(Doctoral Dissertations, William James College).*

Darwin, C. (1871). *The descent of man, and selection in relation to sex.* London: Murray.

Deming, W. E. (1993). *The new economics.* Cambridge: M.I.T.

Deming, W. E. (1994). *The new economics for industry, government, education.* Cambridge: MIT Press.

George, B. (2015). *Discover your true north.* New York, United States: John Wiley & Sons.

Goleman, D. (1998, Nov-Dec). What makes a leader. *Harvard Business Review,* pp. 93-102.

Heifetz, R., Grashow, A., & Linksy, M. (2009). *The practice of adaptive leadership: Tools and tactics for changing your organization and the world.* Boston, MA, United States: Harvard Business Press.

Hines, P., & Butterworth, C. (2019). *The essence of excellence.* S A Partners Publication.

Kanawaty, G. (1992). *Introduction to work study* (4th ed.). Geneva: International Labour Office.

Liker, J. K., & Ogden, T. (2011). *Toyota under fire: Lessons for turning crisis into opportunity.* New York: Mc Graw Hill.

Lombardo, M., & Eichinger, R. (1996). *The career architect development planner* (1st ed.). Korn / Ferry.

Margolis, J. D., & Stoltz, P. G. (2010, Jan-Feb). How to bounce back from adversity. *Harvard Business Review.*

Mercer. (2022). *Global talent trends study 2022: The rise of the relatable organization.* Mercer.

Preece, K., & Beekman, M. (2014, August). Honeybee waggle dance error: adaption or constraint? Unravelling the complex dance language of honeybees. *Animal Behaviour, 94*, 19-26.

Rumelt, R. (2017). *Good strategy/bad strategy.* London, United Kingdom: Crown Publishing.

Senge, P. (2006). *The fifth discipline: The art and practice of the learning organization.* New York: Doubleday.

Sherman, G. D., Lee, A. J., Cuddy, A., Renshon, J., Oveis, C., Gross, J. J., & Lerner, J. S. (2012). Leadership is associated with lower levels of stress. *Proceedings of the National Academy of Sciences -PNAS, 109 (44)*, pp. 17903-17907.

Shingo. (2022). *The Shingo Model* (Vol. Version 14.9). Utah: Utah State University.

Simons, D. J. (2000). Attentional capture and inattentional blindness. *Trends in Cognitive Sciences, 4*(4), 147–155.

Simons, D. J., & Chabris, C. F. (1999). Gorillas in our midst: Sustained inattentional blindness for dynamic events. *Perception (London), 28*(9), 1059 - 1074.

Swart, T., Chisholm, K., & Brown, P. (2015). *Neuroscience for leadership. Harnessing the brain gain advantage.* Basingstoke, United Kingdom: Palgrave Macmillan.

Tisdall, E. K. (2013). The transformation of participation? Exploring the potential of 'Transformative Participation' for theory and practice around children and young people's participation. *Global Studies of Childhood, 3*(2), 183–193.

Ulukaya, H. (2019, May). *The anti-CEO playbook.* Retrieved from TED.com: https://www.ted.com/talks/hamdi_ulukaya_the_anti_ceo_playbook?language=en